Writing for Corporate Video

Related titles from Focal Press

Alternative Screenwriting
  Ken Dancyger

Broadcast Writing
  Ken Dancyger

Corporate Television: a Producer's Handbook
  Ray DiZazzo

Film Scriptwriting: a Pictorial Manual
  Dwight V. Swain with Joye R. Swain

Scripting for Video and Audiovisual Media
  Dwight V. Swain with Joye R. Swain

Writing for Corporate Video

Grant Eustace

Focal Press
London and Boston

Focal Press
is an imprint of Butterworth-Heinemann Ltd

🌐 PART OF REED INTERNATIONAL P.L.C.

First published 1990

© **Grant Colin Eustace 1990**

British Library Cataloguing in Publication Data

Eustace, Grant
    Writing for corporate video.
    1. Video recording scripts. composition
    I. Title
    808.066

    ISBN 0-240-51295-2

Library of Congress Cataloging in Publication Data

Eustace, Grant.
    Writing for corporate video/Grant Eustace.
        p. cm.
    Includes bibliographical references and index.
    ISBN 0-240-51295-2
    1. Television authorship. 2. Industrial television–Authorship
I. Title.
PN1992.7.E97   1990
808'.066791–dc20   90-3414
                                            CIP

Phototypeset by Scribe Design, Gillingham, Kent
Printed and bound in Great Britain by Page Bros. Ltd, Norwich, Norfolk

Foreword

A good corporate television programme must have a good script. It's as simple – and complicated – as that. And as the business has burgeoned, our audiences have become more discriminating: they are well beyond being charmed simply by seeing their colleagues on screen. High quality scripts always were important; they are now essential. Grant clearly knows this, and his book provides an excellent introduction to the work

One cannot teach how to be a writer, but one can show how the industry works, how the scriptwriting should be approached, and how to avoid the pitfalls. This Grant does, with a great deal of perception. Obviously based on hard-won experience, his observations are full of good sense. What's more, the book is written in a style to match: it is direct, well illustrated, and easy to read.

From basic information on who does what, to creating television that tingles. It's all covered. Of course, some of the issues could be debated far into the night; the use of humour, for instance. A tricky area when it isn't always clear *whose* fancy you're trying to tickle. However, part of the interest of working in corporate television is precisely that it does have issues to debate. It is a comparatively young industry, and its scriptwriters have an exciting role to play in developing it.

And whatever the challenge, Grant's experience is worth listening to.

Jean Smith
Chair, Writers' Group
International Visual Communications Association

Preface

Writing for video is simple. You only need knowledge of the medium, an understanding of people, acute listening and analytical skills, wide-ranging experience, an organized mind, a jackdaw memory, your fair share of imagination and the ability to write.

Useful bonuses are realistic timescales, a producer and director sympathetic to the written word and its creator, and a client clear in his or her objectives and familiar with the strengths and weaknesses of video.

Unfortunately, that complete combination is not much more common than a tap-dancing stick insect. So this book has been written to help.

It can only supplement such gifts as a writer might already have. But as it is based on practice rather than theory, it should be able to substitute for much of that valuable but extremely dispiriting process, learning by one's mistakes.

As the book's title makes plain, it is aimed at corporate video. In this context, 'corporate' is a shorthand adjective for any non-broadcast video that deals with factual content. It may be entertaining as well, but entertainment is not its primary purpose.

In fact, it is very often truly corporate bodies which need and fund these videos. Hence their generic name. But the umbrella term includes the many organizations (such as the armed services, the emergency services, departments of state, museums and charities) which are not commercial but have just as much need for videos. Virtually all the aspects of writing for video discussed here will apply equally to all of them, however much the scripts themselves may vary.

The word 'video' is itself shorthand in those circumstances where the material is not being originated on video equipment.

There was a time when the quality of film was so markedly better than video that even a layman would notice. With all the work that has been put into video development, that gulf has now been virtually bridged. There are nevertheless occasions when the choice will be made to shoot on film, and sometimes – usually because of the size of the viewing auditorium – to project on film, too. The effect on the writer is negligible, and as a result I have used the word 'video' all the time.

I have also used it most of the time to cover a rather different variant, when the visual material is originated on 35 mm slides. There could be good reasons for choosing to do that, and the subject is therefore looked at in more depth later on (Chapter 3). But from the point of view of the writer, only a few aspects of the job change. Where 'video' is used, the reader can take it that there are no differences that affect the script.

I am in need of one other piece of shorthand, but sadly the language does not possess it yet. I am no sexist. Corporate video would be the wrong field to be in if I were. I know personally a good number of female writers and directors, and increasingly producers and clients as well. I know of many more. Indeed, most other areas of business have a long way to go before they are anywhere near as equal. But that creates a language hazard for this book.

The accurate 'he or she' can become tedious to read after a time, and the convolutions of the text to avoid it can be just as tiresome. 'They' is inappropriate to what is usually a lone individual. So I have tried to move between 'he' and 'she', not as a whim but as an attempt to maintain parity.

If the scales still end up tilted towards 'he', I can only ask that lady readers accept that mentally I am viewing situations from where I am standing, and have just relaxed from the egocentric 'I' into the general-case 'he'. No offence is intended by the word, any more than there is in the convention of the corporate address 'Dear Sirs'.

The emphasis of the book is placed squarely on the practical side of video writing. All of the suggestions I make are therefore of the 'do as I do' school: if they have not worked for me in practice, I do not make them. All of the cautionary tales are included because they happened.

The examples which flesh out what I am saying are also real, and come from three main sources. They are from script projects that I have personally worked on. They are from videos I have seen which were written by others. Or they have been told to me by people in the profession on whose evidence I can rely.

In some instances it is obvious which is which. In most cases it is irrelevant, and I have not bothered to differentiate. It is not my intention thus to take the credit for writing in which I had no hand. It is in the nature of corporate video that the viewer will usually have no idea who wrote it. I trust any writer whose good work I am citing anonymously will take it as it is intended: as a professional compliment.

The responsibility for any opinions expressed in the pages that follow is mine. But I have sought the views of others during the preparation of this book, and I am grateful to them for their time and their thoughts. I am particularly indebted to Paul Swan, Managing Director of Spectrum Communications; Gabrielle Staples, Head of Training and Motivation, and Andrew Fitch, Head of Video, at Purchasepoint; Adrian Arnold, Production Director, and Mike Boxall, Course Development Manager, at Interactive Information Systems; and the actor (and masterly video voiceover) Martin Jarvis.

I would also like to thank Gerald Bowthorpe, Deputy Managing Director of the OCS Group; Michael Aha, Personnel Director, Data General Europe; and Andrew J. Buchanan, General Manager, Ettington Park Hotel, for their willingness to let me reproduce in the appendices scripts which I have written for them.

Contents

1

Who, and Why
The writer's place in the video team, and the case for video

The production of any video is a team process. The writer will probably not be as prominent a member as in a play for the theatre or for radio, but the script is still all-important. The writer will contribute much, if not all, of the framework, and will write the great majority of the words.

A director can always fail to realize a good script's full potential; but the more workmanlike it is to begin with, the more likely it is to survive. (Witness the way Shakespeare's plays continually rise above the most misguided directorial excesses.) Even the best directors, however, are hard put to it to make much of mediocre material. The old maxim about silk purses and pigs' ears still applies.

On the writer's shoulders, therefore, rests much of the responsibility for success. This is despite the fact that he or she is not – as in purely creative writing forms – the originator of the process. It is also possible that by the time other hands have worked on the script after him, he may barely recognize the end product as deriving from his work. No matter. The role is still vital.

It fits into the following structure:

1

This is the ideal situation. It has at the production level three individuals on an equal footing dealing with a fourth person for whom the video is being made. With the need for some point of reference for this book, the presumption throughout is that something approximating to this structure exists.

The fact that reality can be far removed from this ideal will be addressed in a moment, but it is as well to start with the roles of each of the four as they ought to be.

The client is the person who is commissioning the video on the basis of some identified need. If the production team is an in-house one, he is no less a client in the part he or she has to play. From the writer's point of view, this has three elements: briefing the project; acting as the source of supplementary information during the scripting process; and signing off the final version of the script as acceptable (and accepted).

The writer comes in two main forms. He works full-time in the same production outfit as the director or producer, or he is a freelance brought in by one of them (or much less commonly, by the client) on a script-by-script basis.

I am bound, as a freelance, to believe that to be the preferable system, but in fact each has its advantages from the client's point of view. Lines of communications are shorter to an in-house writer. She should have a closer rapport with the director, and be more able to reflect the style of the production company (which may have been what influenced the client to choose it in the first place). A freelance, on the other hand, ought to be able to justify her position by bringing to bear specific experience or a fresher approach.

Classically the director and producer divide their work in the film-making sense. The director physically makes the video, and the producer holds the pursestrings and runs the logistics. In practice, many of the producer's tasks are taken over by the director, and the producer oversees progress and liaises with the client more in the manner of an account director in an advertising agency.

This is a variation on the ideal which presents no problems. Nor does the complete disappearance of the producer as a separate individual, with direction and production fully integrated in one person.

There is nothing to be wary of, either, in another – admittedly unusual – change in the structure that looks like this:

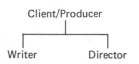

Indeed, it has the solid advantage that the client must already have at least an interest in and an understanding of video to be able to double up on roles in this way. (In one instance I have experienced, he even provided some footage for the video taken with his personal camera.)

Less happy is a re-arrangement, quite common in – among other places – a military environment, that results in this:

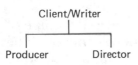

The drawback with this structure is that the client is not likely to understand fully the *video* needs of the script. At the very least the director will have to take on a more or less covert role as script editor. A particularly strong-willed client may fight bitterly over every word he has sweated to write, all of which in any case he believes are essential.

As with many such instances, long-term improvement lies down the road of education. It could be, after all, that the client is the only person with the detailed knowledge to be able to write the script. (A professional writer with an agile enough brain should be able to think his way into most subjects, but the budget or the rules may preclude one. In any case, in a strictly hierarchical organization like an army, it is perhaps less than wise to tell a client senior to you that he is not the best person for the job.)

What is vital in the short term, however, is that the client is made aware of how his words will be used, and so how they should be written. The apt solution proposed in one armed service was to make a video to show such client/writers what is required of them.

Increasingly common is another arrangement that occurs within many large organizations that set up their own video units:

Client
|
|
|
Writer/Producer/Director

The compression of all three roles into one person is not always helpful. The management of the separate tasks is bad enough just in its time aspects. More difficult still is remaining sufficiently objective about one's work, so that the director can fulfil his function of criticizing the script in order to improve it.

Many readers will nevertheless already be in this position or one day find themselves in it. I can offer no magic cure. I can only highlight the hazard. How well it is overcome is dependent on the personality of the individual, and the pain involved in giving birth to any one script and the consequent reluctance to amend it.

It may be that, for important or just large projects, the line of least aggravation is to take a second professional opinion. The client is unlikely to be useful in this respect: it will need another director or writer. Unless you're lucky, such service will not come for nothing. But it will come more cheaply than a commissioned script, and could well be cost-effective measured against the need for a quality product.

Even an unprofessional opinion can help. A spouse or friend may well be totally unversed in the conventions of the medium. But their instinctive reactions can at least make us justify what we have written. 'I find this section very complicated.' 'Why have you dealt with it in that order?'

It is precisely the sort of amateur but highly beneficial criticism that my wife has applied to this text.

If those options are not available, the alternative of time will have to be tried. The longer we can leave our own script draft unread, the easier it will be to make changes.

Words hot off the word processor are perfect. After all, we've just written them. Even a day later, let alone across a weekend, their deficiencies become more visible. It sounds like a luxury to let each full draft of a script sit that long. But it is an unusually self-critical person who can muster the necessary objectivity in less time.

The writer, even in the singleton role defined as ideal, needs to tread carefully in three other sets of circumstances. One is when an extra layer is added to the structure:

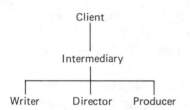

This is fortunately not too common, and most likely to be met in a marketing case, where the intermediary is the client's advertising agency.

It generates several difficulties. On the way down, the client's wishes are already being interpreted before they reach the production team. The intermediary may also want to add in creative input of his or her own (without necessarily being especially competent in the video form). On the way back up, the script can easily be doctored on its journey to the client. And what are in effect two clients have to be convinced in succession about the script.

The only practical advice is: talk to the client directly at some point before committing to the final script, to confirm what you have been told indirectly. And persuade the producer to arrange that the script is presented once, to client and intermediary jointly. You won't always be successful in either case. If you're not, be warned. The process could become more drawn out.

The same effect on the writer is produced by this re-organization:

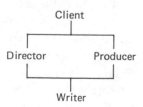

This is not likely to be a conscious move to keep you at arm's length from the client. It can arise simply from the logistical difficulty of getting people with busy diaries together at the same moment. Its effect, however, is the same as in the previous instance – the information the writer receives is filtered, and can easily become distorted as a result.

The solution is the same as well. At some point before the script is delivered, cross-check any grey areas with the client in person if you possibly can. Face to face is best, but even a telephone call will help.

There is one other circumstance in which this structure with the writer at the bottom is simply a reflection of his or her position. Training videos often have no independent existence, but are part of a much wider package of elements with which the writer is not involved. The parameters and treatment are defined by this complete package, and thus already decided by the time the writer is briefed. All that has to be done is to put the body on a skeleton designed by someone else.

It is the nearest equivalent in corporate work to writing an episode for a television series where the main characters are already well established – although with arguably even less room to manoeuvre. It usually applies when the writer is needed for a specific skill such as writing dialogue.

The last of the organizational pitfalls is occasionally the most wearisome of all. The ideal client is one person. But in the corporate field, hardly anyone seems to have (or even to want) the authority to act as sole arbiter for the video. In an extreme case, you sit wondering where to put yourself during the briefing meeting while two directors of the client company shout abuse at each other for their opposing views.

Or the approval process for a delivered script needs five or more inputs from people who can never be marshalled together at the same place at the same time. And then still needs input from their boss, who will overturn half of the committee's decisions.

Or just one page of a 35-page script is sent to the Chairman for his approval because it mentions him. (Of course, despite that lone page's being grotesquely out of context, he felt he would not be doing his job without making a change. So the script came back with the line 'the Bank's policy' altered in his own spidery handwriting to 'policy for the bank' (sic). For decisions of such great moment are people paid six-figure salaries.)

These ought to sound like made-up examples. I just wish they were.

No writer can hope to change the decision-making chain or internal politics of a client. But it is as well to be alive to them, because any lumpiness in this respect (as with any deviations from the ideal team structure) could presage problems at some stage with the script. As with most problems, identifying them or the possibility of them early makes them less disconcerting if they do arise.

And the picture is by no means completely black. There are clients out there, large as well as small, who keep the decision-making quorum down to a maximum of two people, who demand little rewriting because the original brief is so good and yet who are unstinting in their praise when they like what you deliver.

Getting paid as well by people like that feels like a bonus. It reminds you why you choose to write corporate videos.

That the client should have a corporate video has been taken as read in this consideration of roles in its production. 'Why a video?' should not, however, go unasked.

Questioning the reason for a video may seem a little like biting the hand of the goose that lays the golden eggs (as Sam Goldwyn reputedly phrased it). But a writer is a professional. And a professional should flag the fact, however circumspectly, when the considerable cost and effort of a video looks as if it might not be justified.

That will in any case happen only in isolated cases. The most important function of the 'Why' question is to focus the writer on to how the script can draw on a video's strengths.

The principal failing of video, as those paying for it see it, is that it does not act like a shotgun. It works like a rifle. Scattering pellets roughly in the right direction will achieve little. In the words of one producer, 'a good video does very little extremely well'.

The direct relevance of this to the writer is that the target, the audience for the video, needs to be defined by the client as accurately as possible. The narrower the definition, the more likely that the target will be hit.

Yet some clients will want to show this expensively produced beast to customers, employees, shareholders, trade unions, politicians, investors and probably to their family and pets as well. They then expect the writer to script it so that it works just as effectively for all of them.

In a few instances, that can still be done; but nowhere near as often as they would like. The limitations of video in this respect may need to be stressed – if only to get one of those audiences given the pole position.

More significantly, the aim of the video requires to be thought through with some care. Individual members of the audience will pick up particular details of interest to them. But to judge a video effective, all of them must get the same fundamental message from it.

It is sometimes called the clipboard question. If you stand at the door with your clipboard as the audience files out after watching the video, what is it that all of them should be saying in answer to: 'What did you get out of that video?'

This concept of the thread holding the whole script together is integral to its success. It will therefore re-appear in later chapters, and its significance will be fully underlined then. Suffice it to say here that – from the writer's angle – that single message is effectively the bullet we must put into the rifle.

Even if the narrow targeting of the best videos can be seen as a disadvantage, most people are already aware of some of the medium's unequivocally positive facets. The message is consistent every time it is heard, for example. So is the quality: it does not rely on the variable skill of individuals to deliver it well. And a video is convenient to transport and easy to use.

But all of that applies to a glossy brochure, and it can have pictures, too. The video comes into its own in two other respects.

First, the pictures are moving. That is not as fatuous a statement as it might seem, because sadly the movement on screen often ends up being minimal. The headquarters building can be as impressive in a photograph as on video. The list of blue chip customers might even be better on the page, although it could be given life by being scrolled up the screen.

The virtue on video of a management tree or a diagram is only that it can be built up stage by stage, in the manner of a reveal on an overhead projector slide. Otherwise it might as well stay on the page.

But show an aircraft in flight, or a carnival, or vehicles, or people interacting, or manufacturing processes, or nature at its more violent, and the video image is unbeatable.

Second, watching a video should in part be an experience for which there is no substitute, or at least no practical one. That means it must take the audience where they cannot otherwise go.

Sometimes that is literally so. Hall 2 of the International Congress Centre in Berlin transforms from an open space to an auditorium when an enormous section of apparent ceiling, with seats on its upper side, is lowered to the floor. The process takes half an hour. As a gripping spectacle it is a poor second to watching grass grow. But film it in short bursts, and the 30 minutes compresses to a dramatic 20 seconds, and the video is doing what only it can do.

When the Birmingham Convention Centre existed only as a model, a similarly impossible effect was achieved by a snorkel camera that went into the model and made it appear life-size. A plan was made to come alive.

Rare occasions – such as the Passion Play at Oberammergau – can be captured on video for millions to see in the intervening ten years before it is staged again. Or a never-repeated event such as a product launch is there in the future as unarguable testimony to how such events can be mounted.

Filming micro-nature at high levels of magnification is another example of the otherwise physically impossible.

These are special cases, although significant ones. But there are many other ways we can plan to use the video to its best advantage. We can take people where it is dangerous to go – close to machinery or even inside manufacturing processes, for example, or down mines and into quarries, or up on to the roofs of tall buildings.

We can take them where it is extremely difficult to go, such as into the cockpit of a manoeuvring fighter aircraft.

We can let them see places in ways which would be extremely expensive for every member of the audience, such as when viewed from a helicopter.

We can show them places to which privacy or security might otherwise deny them access. (A bank's recruitment video squandered one such opportunity, by opening the heavy steel outer vault door but then keeping the barred inner one locked.

Surely the camera could at least have been poked through the bars to show the bags of money that were being talked about?)

Most obviously, perhaps, and sometimes most importantly, we can telescope travelling time to a few seconds by transporting the audience to wherever we want in the comfort of their chairs.

If you are encouraging businessmen to go to the Arab Gulf, you bring the Gulf to them. If you are marketing an international once-a-year trade fair, your potential customers can experience it all the year round in their own countries. If the company has twenty locations spread around the country, we can call at all of them and never set foot outside head office.

For internal communication inside large organizations, the video can achieve the reverse of the last example. It can take head office, and the key people in it, to the most far-flung subsidiary in the world for simply the cost of the video cassette making the journey. The alternatives, such as the Managing Director spending a solid month travelling, do not even leave the starting post.

In a training context this characteristic of video is immensely helpful. Rarely do we want to set up a live training environment when real customers are present. Even less do we want customers about if we would like to demonstrate mistakes and disasters. Nor is it straightforward to simulate badly injured people, or civil disturbance, or repair work underwater, let alone on a regular basis.

Yet a video can do any of those easily – with the extra benefit that we can replay it and analyse it as many times as we want.

Used properly, therefore – correctly targeted, and exploiting its strengths – the video is without peer. But even the best of intentions can go awry, if the ways in which the medium achieves its results are not fully understood. That is the subject of the next chapter.

2

Images and Sounds
The core elements of video, and the relationships between them

To talk in terms of 'a video' – that is, of the finished article as a single entity – can be misleading. A video in its finished state is like many other forms of creative work, an amalgamation of elements – although no seams will show when the job is done properly.

Some of the elements are purely technical, and so must be left to the director. From the point of view of the writer, there are four. The primary pair are words and pictures; sounds and music are in support.

That may appear to be merely a statement of the obvious. But since it is of fundamental importance, it is as well to spell it out. The effectiveness of a corporate video depends to a large extent on getting the balance right between those elements, and above all between the primary pair. It does not always happen.

The very fact of needing a written script leads those who are already biased towards words to place all the emphasis on them, and end up with too many. This overkill is then made worse if those words are written by someone who also does not appreciate there are differences between prose and speech.

The result is much closer to a textbook than a script. Watching a video made from it can be a deadly experience. The audience is battered with a continuous flow of words that at times bears no relation to the pictures, at others simply duplicates them and frequently provokes complete mental indigestion.

Yet such writers are not usually stupid people. They drive cars. So they are aware how much information the eye can take into the brain from a mass of road signs and other rapidly changing visual cues, and how quickly.

They know what a frown or a yawn or a shake of the head means around the table at a meeting, without any need for verbal explanation.

Most significantly, they see films in the cinema or on television. So they should have realized by now how much of a story can be told and how much tension sustained by mainly visual means. In the pivotal scene in *The Third Man*, for example, where Harry Lime appears for the first time, nearly one and a half minutes of film contain just the one word, 'Harry', spoken twice.

Or consider another striking instance, from a more modern film. At the end of the German-language *Colonel Redl*, the framed army officer of the title is handed back his pistol: he is offered suicide in preference to a court martial. From the moment the gun is put on Klaus Maria Brandauer's desk to his managing to force the muzzle against his temple and press the trigger, 4¾ minutes elapse. In all that time there is one line of dialogue – and the mood achieved is that of an overtightened violin string quivering just before it snaps.

Yet face the language enthusiasts with the task of writing a corporate video script, and still the words pour out in a torrent. The effectiveness of pictures is forgotten. The virtue of the pause is ignored. A radio skill such as pacing has never been noticed. (Listen to Alistair Cooke, who scripts himself, as a classic practitioner.)

Words come to be measured by quantity, not quality. Offer clients a finished script with only the necessary amount of words, and you prompt remarks like 'You obviously aren't being paid by the word'. Even a professional writer can watch a corporate video and say, with genuine surprise in her voice, 'There really aren't very many words, are there?'

Those of a strongly visual persuasion, however, can stumble just as easily by moving too far in the opposite direction. They risk losing sight of the functional nature of every corporate video. This is not art for art's sake. The much-loved 'moody' shot – the splendiferous computer graphics – the devices that lie temptingly to hand in the editing suite – all these, and all the other visual techniques and tricks, are merely self-indulgent unless they are harnessed to meeting the client's requirement.

In 88 instances out of 90 (citing my own experience), that will mean a planned package of spoken words.

Yet the all-pictures school is not usually ignorant, either. They know that Orson Welles caused thousands of Americans to believe that this planet was being invaded, simply through the power of a play broadcast on radio.

They have experienced a theatre audience dazzled by the verbal acrobatics of Tom Stoppard's dialogue, or by the elegant wit of Oscar Wilde's.

They might even remember being read stories as a child, and be able to recall how vivid were the dragons and wolves and tank engines that were in fact only words on a page, being spoken.

These same people will nevertheless yearn in their hearts to shoot in grainy black and white with two-minute-long silent tracking shots. They envy the anarchy of pop videos. They will start work with a storyboard rather than a script. (One of the great Hollywood directors, Howard Hawks, when asked if he used a storyboard, replied 'Never heard of one'. There could be a moral there.)

If you are really unlucky, you can even encounter a client who greets you with 'What do you want a scriptwriter for? You just point the bloody camera at it, don't you?' (This is a sanitized version of the incident. The actual expressions used were even more revealing of the man.)

One of the key tasks in corporate video is thus to reconcile these two extreme positions. While the writer is by no means the only person who can do it, he or she is often in the best position to strike the right balance. It is not an outrageous generalization to say that the client will usually want to use too many words, and the director to concentrate on the pictures. The good corporate writer should take possession of the middle ground between them.

The difficulty is that there is no one answer to what the correct balance is. It is dictated by the subject matter and the objectives in each individual case, and will vary, sometimes markedly, from one video to another.

There are, however, some key principles about words, images and sounds and the relationships between them. As with other such groupings (dwarfs, deadly sins, wonders of the world), there are seven. Together they provide a reliable framework, to which the detailed requirements of any one video can be added.

1. Let the pictures do all they can

They can do a great deal. There is no better proof of the human brain's extraordinary capacity for processing visual images than the fact that we have to ban subliminal advertising. If the eye can detect and the grey cells register a single picture shown for a fraction of a second, we can expect an audience watching a video to be capable of absorbing a lot simply by watching the screen.

Thus we gain nothing by *saying* what can be shown. But the practical rule of thumb derived from the power pictures have is stronger still. It is that the writer should be actively seeking *not* to say things if there is any way they can be visualized, in the literal meaning of the word.

If anything is worth putting money on, it is that the net result of the process of revising a script will be more words. Only very occasionally would you lose that bet: there are some things which clients will feel simply must be said. There will be nowhere near as many extra pictures. So let the pictures make the running initially.

This is perhaps the most important mental adjustment that a writer coming to video from books or radio or advertising copy has to make. A script is no less a script because half or more of the words are describing pictures.

The director will have the final say on that score, naturally enough, and a shooting script is rarely (if ever) demanded of a writer. The editing, too, will very much dictate the final effectiveness of the visuals. But that does not prevent the writer scripting the overall shape and setting the general tone.

Take the case of a video about the Philippines. The opening sequence showed a national dance, the Singkil, seen in plan view in the manner of Busby Berkeley, and punctuated by colourful and contrasting Philippine scenes. Each of the interpolated shots lasted less than a second, their frequency dictated by the beat of the bamboo poles struck together as part of the dance. The finished version stuck very closely to the original script, which read:

Sound of Singkil
Bamboos seen from directly above
Music added to sound of bamboos, camera begins to move upwards
Sharp sound and picture cuts, alternating new images with increasingly
high view of bamboos, still from directly above, such as:
– Jeepney in busy environment
– Poolside party
– Typical food, such as shellfish or tropical fruits
– Fiesta
– Rural scene, e.g. Carabao pulling plough
– Close-up of golf ball, driven off tee
Still seen from directly overhead, the people operating the bamboos are
now visible, but as yet no dancers
Pull through dancers

The director still had any amount of room to place his own stamp
on it; but the writer had marked out the path. As he should.

What pictures can do particularly well is establish place
economically. (The concept of 'economy', achieving the maximum
amount with the minimum means, is an important one. It runs
throughout this book.) What takes a novelist a paragraph or two
or three is achieved on video in an instant. The audience's
memory bank draws on its accumulated knowledge and experience, and in seconds a policeman tells us it is Britain, and Tower
Bridge that it is London. In the same way, there is only one Eiffel
Tower, and Taj Mahal, and Golden Gate Bridge and Sydney
Opera House.

These are clichés, to be sure, but no less usable for that. The
rule (like its more famous companion saying. 'it's not what you
say, it's the way that you say it') is that 'it's not what you shoot but
the way that you shoot it'.

Such scenes were ideal, for example, in a British Airways
training video aimed at ground staff who do not necessarily see
the more glamorous end of airline life. This, the pictures said, is
why we are in business. This is where our customers go.

We are not in any case limited just to the workaday tourist
vocabulary of the travelogue. The lorry and trailer combination
used in mainland Europe is unlikely to be confused with the long,

shiny rigs on the US Interstate. A boat on the Rhine will not be
mistaken for one on the Ganges. A beach in the Bahamas and the
beach in Brighton have little more than the sea in common, and
even that is a different colour.

More usefully still, we can establish a detailed location with the
same economy. Whether we are in an office or a cathedral or an
airport departure lounge, whether we are on a farm or a building
site is immediately obvious.

Similarly, in a supermarket training video, the customers
moving around the store were located within it simply by the
products they were putting in their trolley.

Even finer differences are just as easy. If it is a bar rather than a
public house or a restaurant, we can see that immediately. A good
hotel or a shabby one is clear from just a few telling visual details.
And changing from one of these to another is equally
trouble-free, just as is changing from day to night.

Insert people into whatever location we have established, and
their clothes and their behaviour tell us their jobs and relative
status. We can understand without difficulty their age, what is
taking place and even what period we are in.

Go in closer and we can learn at a glance much about an
individual's personality. If they are in a good humour, or bored,
or tired or unwell or drunk, we can see it.

The value of this is seen most notably, perhaps, in feature films.
The good ones – despite considerable time at their disposal – often
delineate people using very few words. In *The Magnificent Seven*,
the scene introducing and firmly establishing the character played
by James Coburn lasts nearly four minutes. Coburn himself has
five words of dialogue.

It is, nevertheless, just as important in the corporate context.
Time is almost always limited, if only because of the audience's
capacity to sit and be receptive. So anything that allows us to pass
on information with little effort is helpful.

At a practical scripting level, therefore, if a hotel is in a splendid
setting, show it, don't say it. Seeing a machine at work, or a
manufacturing process as it happens, is more useful than
describing it. Bar and pie charts are much more graphic than
spoken statistics. The reactions on people's faces say much more
than words telling us how they feel. And the use of recognizable
locations helps to keep the video plausible.

The last statement, especially pertinent in a training context, can admittedly cause problems. Although those normally have administrative rather than creative fallout, a writer may well need to take them into account.

BMW, for example, has distinctive showrooms for its cars which any dealer's employee could identify instantly as only a studio mock-up, if that is what is on the screen. So for a customer-care video, a real dealer's showroom had to be used. But real showrooms are busy six days a week, and real customers would not take kindly to the disruption of filming. Ergo, the production had to be shot on a Sunday.

For banks, the solution to not disturbing customers by filming at weekends is then overwhelmed by considerations of security in the branch being used as a set. So at least one British clearing bank has built a permanent replica branch in a studio at one of its training centres. Any procedural training video is thus always visibly in the correct environment.

When talking about letting pictures do all the work they can, there is one important caution. The audience's memory bank must indeed contain the information that enables them to interpret what they are seeing.

The difference between the skylines of Denver and Atlanta, say, might be immediately clear to an American audience; but it would only say 'large American city' to most Europeans.

The registration letter on a British car number plate dates it immediately – but only to Britons. A German number plate identifies the town of registration – but only if you are familiar with the system.

Differences can be just as sharp even within the same country. The concourse of a particular London station will be instantly recognizable to the commuters who use it every day. But to someone in the North of England or Scotland, it will only say 'railway station'.

Stereotypes appear to be an attractive shortcut to solving this problem, but are risky in this respect as in others. In an exercise on a video writing training course, delegates latch on quickly to the fact that the video, about tourism to part of the UK, is to be shown in the US. They consistently suggest showing 'a typical American tourist' as a thematic device. It is only when asked what they mean that they realize they have no idea what such a person would actually look like.

For good reason. Short of unacceptable caricature, no such

person exists. And no audience would therefore recognize that visual image if it were given it.

And no director will thank a writer for proposing a visual motif that is incapable of being put into practice.

The essentially factual content of corporate videos also demands extra thought. If we are setting out purely to entertain, a little audience uncertainty may not matter. Indeed, we may be able to exploit it. But not in a corporate video.

Unless we are careful, we end up taking familiar places, objects or actions for granted. It is a particular danger when the writer is an expert or specialist.

When that happens, we can present pictures that only make sense if the target audience knows more than in fact it does. Such pictures confuse. If we do it deliberately, to achieve a specific effect, it must only be momentary and fully in control. It should never happen by default.

In an otherwise intelligent and well-mounted video at the McDonald Observatory in Texas, for example, a technician was seen in the act of what looked like loading ice into a box attached to the side of a large telescope. No explanation was offered. Nor was there any internal logic in the sequence of pictures to guide us. As a result, the audience's attention was diverted by wondering what on earth it could be looking at. Someone sitting behind me said 'I guess he's fixing the cocktails'.

Such instances serve to underscore one of the absolute fundamentals of corporate video writing that does not just apply to pictures. The moral is simply: know your (client's) audience.

Lest it should seem, from praise of the visual image, that I have suddenly joined the all-pictures school, let me balance that impression immediately with a second principle.

2. Words are best for ideas

Cinema enthusiasts may well bridle a little at this one. Certainly, feature films have tackled many themes of considerable substance: the nature of love, of honour, of fear, the futility of war, the power of the Mafia, the capacity of human beings to destroy themselves and others. And they make ample use of visual means to do so.

But they have upwards of 90 minutes in which to do it. In the case of epics like the full version of *Lawrence of Arabia*, they have 216 minutes. The corporate video audience does not have that amount of patience, and rightly so.

The contrast can be extreme. In the long opening sequence of *Once Upon a Time in the West*, a group of men waits at a flyblown railroad station. The roving camera, picking up eccentric and revealing details, relates to us the men's boredom and impatience and much of their individual characters. We are as expectant as they are by the time the train eventually arrives. Who can it be they are waiting for?

It is excellent cinema – but it would be hopelessly profligate corporate video. In that length of time we need to be fully to grips with the meat of our subject matter. Words are our principal means of doing that.

In fact, some of the most memorable moments even in cinema are when a few words encapsulate an idea. Humphrey Bogart's 'It doesn't take much to see that the problem of three little people don't amount to a hill o'beans in this crazy world' at the end of *Casablanca*. The hunchback Charles Laughton's triumphant shout of 'Sanctuary!' from high up on Nôtre Dame. The 'Make my day' that so closely defines *Dirty Harry*.

But there are better models elsewhere for the corporate writer in this respect. There are good public speakers who have only words to transmit their ideas. 'An iron curtain has descended across the Continent.' 'It is the unpleasant and unacceptable face of capitalism.' 'I have a dream.'

There are advertising ideas that stand the test of long exposure. 'A diamond is forever.' 'The world's favourite airline.' 'There are perhaps a dozen incredible places you must see in the Orient. One of them is a hotel.'

There are news stories whose pictures were made much more memorable by words. The true import of the Apollo 11 landing on the moon came with 'That's one small step for a man, one giant leap for mankind'. The first haunting television pictures from an Africa stricken by drought showed us the problem; but the idea that we could help was expressed in Band Aid and Comic Relief.

At first glance such examples may not appear to have much connection with corporate video writing. But their relevance is two-fold.

First, they demonstrate again the value of economy: a great deal of content expressed in a succinct form. What is a virtue for pictures is just as much of one with words.

Second, every corporate video worth its salt has some central idea at its heart, directly related to the clipboard question in the last chapter. Most of the time that idea needs to be articulated, to ensure that every member of the audience has grasped it.

For example, a naval training video about minesweeping was correctly concerned with the technical minutiae of its complex subject. The implicit idea all the way through was that the hallmark of the professional sweep deck was skill, speed and safety working in unison.

But that needed to be explicit. That way the welter of detail would have been put into perspective. The audience might have been encouraged to go out and emulate what they had seen. That was, after all, the point of the video.

What was actually said at the end was: 'The procedure for streaming and recovering single Oropesa is essentially the same except that only one sweep wire is streamed from either the port or starboard side.' I don't believe that would light anybody's fire.

Or a second, rather happier example. A vending machine manufacturer wanted to make two points: their equipment was reliable and efficient – but the food it produced was still high quality. Their video went out on the words: 'Systems from the future – standards from the past'.

Or a third. A visually very exciting and otherwise wordless video of how a spectacular car launch was organized concluded: 'In 6 weeks, 70 people using 10 tons of equipment turned an idea into reality.'

Put these first two principles together, and a third emerges quite naturally.

3. Words and pictures should complement, not duplicate, each other

There are a few, very isolated exceptions. A company's name may appear on the screen at the same time as that name is said. Or a training point may be spoken and appear as a caption simultaneously.

But they are still exceptions, and not necessarily the only way of meeting a particular requirement. Saying the company's name but showing its logo, for example, is already moving down the complementary road.

The strengths of words and pictures tend to cancel each other out if they are in direct competition. That is why a script adopting the conventional corporate layout (pictures on one side, words on the other) often has a zigzag look to it. The pictures establish a scene, the words pick up an idea, the next pictures embellish it until more words are needed, and so on.

Thus the words do not run helter-skelter after one another. Even so, they must still be coherent, even without the pictures.

A corporate video has a factual story to tell: it must be complete and hang together before the pictures can be added. It might not be written that way – indeed, should not be written that way – but all the words will have to be approved before the shooting can start.

The only time in a corporate context when words make little sense divorced from the pictures is that rare case, the full dramatization. Rank Training's *Who Killed The Sale?* is a fine example. There, as in every drama script, the words and pictures only work in conjunction with each other.

Pictures, on the other hand, cannot usually stand entirely alone. They normally only become coherent as a whole when linked together with words. This is not to downrate the pictures. It is simply to acknowledge the role of words in corporate video.

One of the most visually innovative directors I have known used to read the words in their entirety before she looked at any visualization. She believed it was pointless thinking about the pictures until the shape and direction of the full narrative was clear to her. That was, and in my view remains, a professional approach.

The words need to include only what is not obvious, however. If, for example, a hotel provides outdoor sports such as fishing, clay pigeon shooting, riding and tennis, it is not adding much to say those exact words over scenes of self-explanatory activity.

This is the sort of area, unfortunately, where you could meet client resistance. The argument will be that duplication will ensure retention of the information. I remain unconvinced that that is true, or that retention is necessary at such a moment, except when it is the hotel's unique selling point. (Unlikely, unless it stands in the centre of a city.)

The most we probably want retained from the video is the thought of the range of outdoor activities offered. Words to that effect are then quite adequately supported by the visuals. Any fishermen or tennis fans will pick up the pictures of their favourite pastime, anyway. Heavier emphasis is not needed.

That is nevertheless typical of the sort of words, superfluous as they may be, that can creep into a script during the revision stages. The principle of words and pictures being complementary is thus easily lost. It is worth defending.

It is best demonstrated in a working script. A computer company with subsidiaries throughout Western Europe used a major success story in one country as a springboard into an internal communications video. The narrative line was to establish the country, then the background to the sale, then the sale itself, and lead on into extracting a general case from the specific one. The script opened this way:

Sunlight on water. Suddenly the bow of a boat breaks into the picture: it is, to those who know, an Amsterdam canal boat. Much of the boat passes the camera before we pan with its movement, then up and beyond it, to see the typical old architecture of a canal-side street.	
Same or similar street, at street level.	NARRATOR Amsterdam, like any other great city, keeps a lot of people busy.
Begin to focus on individuals such as a postman, a street cleaner, a delivery man.	
A busy street. Establish before focusing on a tram driver.	
Merge tram driver with driver of canal boat.	Which is fine for those who have the jobs.
Discover a woman on a canal	

bridge. Focus on her watching
the boat go by. Clearly with
plenty of time on her hands, she
starts to stroll away

But what about those who are
still unemployed?

She continues walking

The Ministry of Social Affairs in
Holland has an ambitious scheme to
link all the available jobs across
the country to those who need them.

Local Ministry of Social Affairs
office, with woman approaching

and we are helping them do it –
installing over the next 18 months
64 systems serving 1600
workstations. . . . .

The director's additions were pictorial. When filming from a boat
on the canals of Amsterdam, he caught two large resting birds
which suddenly took flight, an attractive image. He found welders
working on the raised hull of a canal barge, again a vivid visual,
but also one which was in strong support of the line about keeping
people busy. And the tourist guide in the boat was more animated
(and, let's be honest, prettier) than the driver. So the male-
operated camera picked her out instead.

But the script again determined the overall direction of the
video, and did so by adhering to the idea of words and pictures
used in complementary fashion.

One half of this primary pair, however, has an important
characteristic of its own:

4. The scripted words have to be spoken

Nothing remarkable in that, perhaps. But it is forgotten more
often than it ought to be. An uncomfortably large proportion of
videos is still cursed by narration that consists of written words
read aloud, or dialogue that is nearly literally unspeakable.

The differences between the spoken and written word are sometimes subtle and elusive. Both 'readability' and 'listenability' are tricky to define. At this stage I will just suggest three main strands within the weave, and Chapter 6 will examine the subject in more detail.

The first strand is the nature of dialogue. It is exactly what it says: people talking as if they were in conversation. The words to stress are 'as if'. It is not real.

True conversation is flabby and unstructured, uses far more words than necessary, is constantly revised as it is spoken and is peppered with ums and ahs. It is all right to be part of, but not very inspiring to listen to.

Dialogue will always be artificial to the extent that it must serve a specific purpose. It must be relevant, immediately understandable and not waste time.

But it must still sound real. It must have the rhythm and emphasis and vocabulary and pauses of natural speech. If it does not, actors will find it difficult to speak naturally, and the audience will find it hard to accept. Yet in a training video, say, if the characters appear to be speaking lines rather than talking normally, the plausibility and hence the value is greatly reduced.

We brush for the first time here against a potentially nasty trap, whose jaws wait to close on us in a number of contexts. It is the trap of audience expectations.

Corporate video in most of its forms – marketing, explaining procedures, communicating to employees and so on – has no direct equivalent in domestic television. Audiences, therefore, have no fixed expectations against which to judge it. They can broadly compare production quality, and so will mostly recognize a tacky video when they see it. But then they would probably be able to recognize one of those, anyway.

The closer we move towards the type of product an audience can see nightly on its television screens, however, the greater the pressure to close the gap completely, or risk losing its attention. Use full dramatization, and you are encouraging a direct comparison of like with like.

It is an unhelpful comparison, because drama has the biggest of all television budgets: larger by several factors than the glitziest corporate production.

Much of the effect of that budget discrepancy is outside the writer's control; but the scenario and dialogue through which it is realized are not. If we take a route that invites comparison with television's products, ours must not be found wanting.

The second strand concerns the bread and butter of corporate video, the narrative (or voiceover, as it is just as widely known). It is not dialogue – but nor is it written word. It sits between the two.

In terms of the choice of words, the writer can range more freely. The superlatives of marketing. The gloss of PR. The slick mastery of technical facts. The lyrical descriptions of the travelogue. All these can work as a voiceover, when they would be unacceptably pompous or pretentious when presented as apparently normal conversation.

Nevertheless, that narrative still has to be spoken. The fact that usually a professional (an actor or broadcaster) will speak the words is no excuse for their being difficult to say with fluency and conviction.

They will need, therefore, to be constructed in sentences that place the key elements where the narrator can emphasize them naturally. That means, among other things, sentences that are not too long or burdened with subordinate clauses. 'Convoluted, unhappy sentences' was how one voiceover artist described them.

We must learn the virtue of the crisp, well-placed adjective. We must beware the soggy effect of passive verbs. We must remember that numbers take longer to say than to read. (The Philippines has 7107 islands. Say that aloud, and you hear why the script chose 'more than seven thousand islands'.) We must be alert to the possible pitfalls of alliteration.

In a word, everything we write must be speakable. 'The more it sounds like a pamphlet or a brochure,' one actor said, 'the harder for us to get the script off the ground.'

The last of the three strands is that words need some air between them. In the days when I was trying to win my spurs as a radio playwright, one of the soundest pieces of advice I was given came from an actor very skilled in the medium. It was in response to my beginner's tendency to overwrite. 'Give the actors a chance to breathe,' he said.

Not only the actors, I learned later. The words themselves lose out if they are piled on top of one another like concrete poured down a chute.

A critical difference between the spoken and written word is that readers go at their own pace, but listeners go at ours. We have to give them a break, in both senses of the expression.

Important statements or facts need a little time to be understood and docketed in our brains. The value of writing economically is lost if the audience has no opportunity to absorb one well-chosen phrase before another arrives, and then another. Too few pauses start to chip away quickly at any carefully built framework of words and pictures being complementary.

Readers have an additional advantage. If they find any difficulty with a text, they can go back and read it again. Listeners have no such safety net. They must be able to register what is said first time around, or they are lost.

In part that means putting the words into unambiguous and easily digested units. But it also means breathing spaces between them.

And there is a further consideration still. Is the video to be shown using soundtracks in different languages, as happens frequently in marketing cases? The time taken to speak a script written in English will expand after translation by 10–20% with many West European languages, closer to 100% with Japanese. The running time and edit points of the pictures, however, usually remain the same to cut down cost. A script in English therefore needs to be even leaner when it is scheduled for subsequent translation.

The differences between the ways listeners and readers handle words leads on to the next principle.

5. The words should be heard, not read

There are admittedly three major exceptions to that, but it still holds good for the majority of cases.

The advance that the introduction of talking pictures represented was not simply that the audience could hear the words being spoken. It was also that captions need no longer be an obstacle to smooth story development.

Take the example of one of the classics of silent cinema, Buster Keaton's *The General*. Its use of visuals is brilliant. But there is still a chewy bit in the centre that has to be explained if we are to make sense of the action that follows. The result is three captions in quick succession, of 21, 19 and 14 words. They are not fatal: the quality of the film is too high for that. But they jar, and slow down the plot unhelpfully, as they always do.

It is thus somewhat surprising that there has been a slight drift in corporate video back to captions. Nowadays at least the pictures remain on the screen and are joined by the captions, rather than picture and caption having to alternate with each other. But anyone who watches foreign-language films with sub-titles will know the problem. The writing only needs to be in small print, or too wordy, or shown against the wrong colour background, or viewed on too small a television set, and the words are as much a hindrance as a help.

Add in the corporate video's natural inclination towards facts, and you have a recipe for irritation. The pictures are fighting for the attention of viewers forced to become readers. The ease with which spoken words can be emphasized, compared with the much more taxing process of achieving the comparable effect in writing, also argues strongly in favour of speech.

Captions continue to gain some ground, however. And if they are used judiciously, they do constitute one of the three exceptions to this principle.

'Judiciously' includes using them sparingly, rather than as an alternative to a narrative. One highly effective video showing a product launch behind the scenes had just two caption sequences, one to open and one to close.

'Judiciously' can also include putting them on the screen in an interesting way. This could be rolling up it at an angle in the fashion now associated with *Star Wars*, although it was a device already in use in *Union Pacific* in 1939. Or the words can move across the bottom of the screen like a conveyor belt.

But beware the temptation to have someone speak the text as well. It contradicts the principle of not duplicating. That is bad enough if it happens with words and pictures, but is worse still with two versions of an identical set of words.

Captions are at their best when, brief and clear, they are there to save the audience work. Such a use is establishing quickly the place and the date in a narrative story line. No-one feels patronized at the start of *The Sting* by the pair of captions 'Joliet, Illinois' and 'September 1936'.

Captions can highlight the passage of time in a swift-moving

series, such as occurred in a naval PR film with no voiceover,
which was signposted by captions such as 'Day 2 – 0700'. The
history of Wembley had no voiceover, but just a sequence of
captioned dates.

In a documentary format, captions can support the contribution of the expert who is speaking by giving his or her identity and
position.

These cases do not usually employ captions as complete
substitutes for spoken words. It is a question, again, of balancing
the elements. In the product launch instance there was
spontaneous speech, caught in the fly-on-the-wall manner. In the
naval film there was scripted and acted dialogue.

The second exception to not making the audience read is
when the words are already in the pictures. Newspaper
hoardings, street names, motorway signs, airport indicators,
company names on buildings and ports of registry on the sterns of
ships are just a few of the many single or collected words that can
save us a lot of talking.

But in fact by saying that, we are again overlapping with earlier
ideas. It is the first principle, of letting the pictures do as much as
they can, coupled with the concept of economy.

The third exception is a separate case. Interactive video, which
is considered in more detail in the next chapter, depends for its
success as a training tool largely on the benefit that the trainee is
in control of the pace at which he or she progresses. Providing
text on the screen to be read is thus not a great problem – and for
getting the best out of the system it is often essential.

Up to now we have considered only words coming in through
the audience's ears. There is, however, more to it than that.

6. Sounds are powerful allies

We live in a noisy world. We may regret it, but we cannot ignore it.
It is not a factor only of 'civilization'. Someone long accustomed to
sleeping in a house under an airport flight path can be kept awake
in the countryside by lowing cattle, persistent owls or the wind in
the eaves. Go virtually anywhere, and there is sound – natural or
man-made or both.

The effect of this on a video is that pictures without sounds
seem unreal, and are therefore much less effective. The audience

is only seeing, when it knows it ought to be hearing as well, and feels slightly uncomfortable as a result. It is as if the video has not been finished, or the volume has been turned down.

It does not help if there is a voiceover, but still no normal sounds. That merely draws attention to the unnatural condition of hearing words as if they were being spoken in a soundproof room.

These are negatives to be avoided. But this sixth principle was stated positively, and that is the way to view it. While still young, people learn the meaning of an enormous range of sounds. So we can both strengthen visual images and reduce the time taken to recognize them by adding sounds to them.

The surge in the engine noise gives a more dramatic edge to pictures of an aircraft taking off. The sound of the camera's motor drive lends colour to pictures of models being photographed. The hum of the floor polisher is a natural accompaniment to a cleaner at work, just as sawing and hammering is to a woodworker.

In addition, the contrast between sounds emphasizes the sharpness of a cut between two pictures: a gentle stream followed by the roar of a waterfall, or mechanical diggers on a building site set against a thatcher on a roof.

Sound at its most impressive can even substitute for pictures completely. It is one of the great strengths of radio. Seagulls and waves breaking on a beach. The hubbub of conversation at a party. The clatter of hooves and wheels from a horse-drawn carriage. The crash of breaking glass. All of them put a clear picture into a listener's mind, quickly and economically.

(Not that radio is without its problems. Try using sound to portray the presence of a gunman, and you realize the limitations of the medium. It is not for nothing that the most widely quoted spoof line among radio practitioners is 'This revolver I am holding in my hand is loaded'.)

I take it for granted that the writer will script sound effects when working in radio. In corporate video, however, I used to be cautious of encroaching on what I had learned was the director's patch. Then I worked with a director who used pictures of a busy office and a city-centre street with no ambient sound in them, and who did not recognize that they were lifeless. Long after the script had been signed off, I was asked by the nervous client to write some more words 'because the gaps between them are too long'.

They were not; but they seemed so because of the silence.

Now I will at least suggest specific sounds where I believe they are important.

This is another area where audience expectations are (or should be) determining the flavour of the finished video. Television viewers are so used to sounds matching the pictures that most of them would not be able to tell you after a programme what they had heard. 'It all just seemed normal.' But they could soon tell if they had heard nothing.

The widely used alternative for sound is music. Silent cinema soon realized the extent to which just a single piano could enhance what was up on the screen. In particular it emphasized changes of pace and the waypoints in the narrative line – which are precisely the benefits music bestows on corporate video, too.

Television critics frequently complain about the intrusive nature of background music, and are right to do so. But they would probably notice more if it were not there at all, just as they would in the cinema. Once again it is a question of balance.

The selection of music is even more the director's prerogative than sounds, and the writer is thus usually restricted to suggesting a change of pace or a different type of music at a certain point in the script. The only exception is when a special piece of music is necessary.

The video of a product launch in Barcelona, for example, drew on the pop song of the same name. And the line 'Nobody does it better' from the theme tune for *The Spy Who Loved Me* was used in a hotel group video because the phrase was (at the time) true.

The significance of what is becoming known as the M & E track (for music and effects) is great. In some cases it can make or break the video. It is therefore unfortunate that this is the field in which the writer can exercise least influence.

But awareness of its importance is a good start, and a few M & E additions to the script are certainly worth trying.

The last of the principles links back to one of the strengths of video mentioned in the previous chapter.

7. Moving pictures should show movement

The first 40 seconds of a marketing video made for a major avionics company was a series of breathtaking aircraft images. An airliner taking off. A fighter in high-speed manoeuvres against a bright blue sky. An army helicopter swooping fast and low over the ground. A naval jet being punched off the catapult of an aircraft carrier. (And all given point, incidentally, by an M & E track mixing together the pilots' radio communications and the engine sounds appropriate to each case.)

Not everybody can draw on such photogenic subjects for their videos. But the thinking that they represent is admirable. Solid state electronics may be a technological marvel, but it is visually about as interesting as cheese slices. Consider what it does, however, rather than what it is, and the possibilities for moving pictures grow, and with them the likelihood of getting and keeping the audience's attention.

Another example occurred later in the same video, when the script was dealing with electronics for sonar. Movement was found by showing a sonobuoy being dropped from a helicopter, deploying its parachute and falling into the sea. Then, when underwater signals were being picked up, it was the actions of the sonar operators that were shown. It was supported, again, on M & E, by the measured and slightly eerie pinging sound of sonar.

Whenever, therefore, the subject matter is not very inspiring to look at (such as computers) or just plain static (such as buildings), we need to look for ways to add some movement with more than just a pan of the camera.

Often we simply need people in the scene, operating the computer terminals or punting past the ancient ivy-covered stones. Sometimes we have to specify a shot, such as when a train is actually crossing the bridge.

But even when we are dealing with an inherently mobile subject, the manner in which we show it matters. Take the example of an up-market car-hire company. Drive one car on the road, and so what? We see them like that every day, in their thousands. Put seven cars in an arrowhead formation on an airfield runway, and film them from a helicopter flying a path towards them at an angle of 45 degrees, and you have a memorable moving image. (And, in the terms of the previous chapter, we have also taken the audience where they cannot go.)

Not that budgets need to run to airborne footage, though. Views of the countryside are made less like picture postcards simply by a tractor or someone on horseback or wood being chopped. A building may be impressive already, but it always gains by having people in it. In a harbour, go for the working tug or busy sailing dinghy every time, rather than the stately yacht or the imperceptibly moving cargo ship.

In corporate video there is one particular barbed wire entanglement that is often thrown down in the way of this principle. It is the so-called talking head.

Increasingly we find we have to include one or more individuals talking straight to camera. They can be indispensable experts, or people who 'politically' must be allowed to contribute, or very senior managers who demand their say. It makes no difference. However skilled they are, they all have the capacity to slow up the video irreparably.

Audience expectations are against us here again. Once, a pundit such as A.J.P.Taylor could give fascinating television talks using nothing but his personality and an empty studio. But later generations have been brought up on the likes of David Attenborough on location whispering to camera with a family of gorillas ranged around him. They are not going to be held for very long by the Managing Director pontificating from behind his desk.

That may not be avoidable, but we must still do all we can to script it short. And compensate elsewhere in the video with movement wherever we can.

The importance of these principles cannot be overstated. They define the shape and the impact of any video we have to write. So, before moving on to look at the next key influence, all seven are brought together here:

Let the pictures do all they can
Words are best for ideas
Words and pictures should complement, not duplicate, each other
The scripted words have to be spoken
The words should be heard, not read
Sounds are powerful allies
Moving pictures should show movement

3

A Job to Do

The different functions videos can perform, and variations on the video theme

'The best of luck', one producer said when I mentioned that I intended to define the different functions videos can perform. By that he meant that the lines between them are often blurred. True enough. But that is not necessarily a foregone conclusion. And in any case if we accept the premise that video is a rifle-shot medium, the less blurring, the better.

Indeed, the rapid increase in video making is leading to a much greater potential for audience saturation. There is therefore a strong case for saying that the accurate targeting that goes with a clear-cut function is getting more necessary all the time.

It is a moot point which is the largest single area, but **Marketing** is certainly a contender. Any video aiming to promote the company and its products, or the organization and its activities, is included under this heading. It takes in product launches, public relations and recruitment, among other more traditional marketing roles. It is always targeted outwards.

The subject matter that the client wants to have in such a video is usually clear enough. The problems, if there are any, are likely to arise in defining the audience and the message.

'Once we've made this video, everyone'll want to use it,' one client said. Nothing wrong with that – unless that line of thinking takes charge at the script stage. Then the audience becomes too broad and the message too diffuse: the shotgun problem again. We need to encourage the client to keep his sights on one principal target group.

33

This is easiest in something already tightly focused like a product launch. It is most difficult at the fuzzy end of PR, where 'the public' is the audience.

The well-made marketing video's great strength is its ability in a short time to generate feelings and emotions in the audience in a way that is quite beyond the printed word and all but a very few speakers.

Among videos targeted inwards, **Training** is already big, and is also held by many to be poised for the greatest growth in the future. It ranges from the generally applicable videos from production houses like Video Arts, Rank and Melrose to the very specific internal programmes that companies make for themselves.

The training video's biggest single virtue is its cost-effective flexibility. Groups of any size down to one can benefit from it, and at a time convenient to their working environment – unlike a training course. It can be seen in 2500 different locations (bank branches, for example) at the same time – unlike even an army of trainers. It is consistent in its message and its standard whenever it is seen, which large companies like Marks and Spencer lay great store by. And it can be made to stand alone or work in conjunction with a trainer.

For the writer, one novelty is likely to be the additional member of the production team:

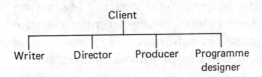

It is common for a training video to have to dovetail into a much larger package that includes live trainers and printed material, and even other videos. When that happens, it is only logical that the programme should be designed as a whole, and that that job should be done by a specialist.

For the writer, the result may well be that a theme or look for the video has already been decided by the time he or she is briefed. Certainly the requirement for a consistent style right across the package will be there. The bonus, to set against any possible loss of room for creative manoeuvre, is that the message will already have been well defined.

An example of the overlap between functional areas is where to place induction videos. Certainly they have a training role to perform. But, to an extent, they are also a tool for communicating internally in the organization, and as such fall into that category as well.

Whichever they are, though, they should always be able to apply one of the fundamental advantages of video. However widespread and varied the organization, it can all be presented to the new trainee within minutes.

The area of **internal communication** just mentioned is also growing. It is undeniably an efficient way to reach all parts of an organization, especially one that is scattered geographically or widely represented abroad. And it will do so with a consistent message. But it is also the most prone to suffering the plague of the talking head, as even talented senior managers turn off their audience by saying too much and moving too little.

The cost of a video 'only' for internal communication also makes it a prime candidate for combining with training. That is unlikely to be a great success. The sum of the total may well end up less than the sum of the parts. That happened in the case of a supermarket group. The internal communication messages (including the Chairman, clearly a frustrated actor, in his office as The Great Manager) were gradually lost in a series of scenarios which became more training-oriented.

The **educational** field is another very large and diverse one. It stretches from the videos produced by public bodies to raise awareness about accident prevention or health, through shows in visitor centres and theme parks to videos in museums. The last of these might deal with just a fraction of a big subject, like the evolution of the dinosaurs, or pre-Raphaelite painting.

Some of them, such as the language-teaching videos produced by BBC English, verge on the televisual. Indeed, some of their programmes are made specifically to be shown on foreign television.

Others tend towards combining marketing with education. Examples include videos made by a bank on how to draw up business plans before asking for banking finance, and by a pharmaceutical company to advise GPs on the use of medicines. If the audience is deliberately kept in the dark about the marketing element, this is a rare instance for the corporate video writer where the ethical ice starts to get a little thin.

This category also contains one of the finest examples that exist anywhere of taking people where they cannot go. *The Dream Is Alive*, shown at the Kennedy Space Center in Florida, has some astonishing footage of both the earth from space and the life of astronauts inside a shuttle. There could be no greater tribute to the makers than the collective gasp from the audience at each successive scene. If NASA were selling space travel, they would get thousands of buyers.

Selling is a field of its own that some audio-visual crystal-ball gazers believe has a great future. At the moment it is used, for example, by large department stores to point out to shoppers what good things they can buy elsewhere in the store. Specialist shops or areas of stores use them to show how particular products perform in practice. Ski equipment is on screen in a sports shop, radio-controlled vehicles in a toy shop and so on.

In very few instances are such videos likely to be of much interest to a writer. One is not needed at all for the 20-second, captioned in-store advertisements (for that is what they really are). The need is scarcely greater when it comes to the few words that accompany product demonstrations, and is not likely to increase with the wider predicted use of video in self-service and after-hours shopping.

So it is to the other main categories of corporate video – marketing, training, internal communication and education – that a writer should be geared.

As the video industry grows, these broad streams are increasingly being sub-divided. The annual awards of the International Visual Communications Association, for example, treat attitudinal and motivational training separately from practical training. The IVCA also gives separate prizes for recruitment, public relations and corporate image, and creates a specific heading of corporate health and safety in addition to that of internal communications. Education has its own award, but with additional ones for medicine and public welfare and safety.

If these narrower definitions help the client to be clearer in his mind what he is seeking to achieve, all well and good. They support the rifle approach. But from the point of view of the writer – and of this book – it is the distinctions between the four umbrella functions that are the most significant.

For some purposes, one of three variations on the theme of video could be appropriate. At least two have just as much need of a writer's services.

Until high-definition television emerges as a commercial product, nothing will grab the attention at a trade fair, exhibition or conference like a **videowall**. This is an array of screens, typically in a square of four up and four across, although other combinations are possible.

This arrangement is expensive to produce. But it has very high impact. Its chief advantage apart from size is that those screens can show either one large picture or a combination of smaller ones, which can be either complementary or contrasting.

A naval PR videowall, for example, used sixteen screens. Among other permutations, it had: eight and eight split vertically; eight and eight split horizontally; twelve with four at the side; twelve with four at the bottom; four mini-squares of four; and fifteen the same and one separate. The sort of split being employed was between the people inside the ship operating weapon systems, and the weapons themselves firing. Another was of different actions taking place simultaneously on an aircraft carrier's flight deck.

If a videowall is used in a closed environment like a conference, where the audience is captive, the complete programme will probably still need to be scripted with a voiceover. In an open environment like an exhibition stand, with a rotating audience of passers-by, it is much more likely to go just for a strong M & E track. (That was what the naval example did.)

Either way, the videowall capitalizes on the visually arresting results of its design, and the writer must therefore think even more in visual terms. The collaboration between writer and director will need to be closer. In most cases that do not require a spoken soundtrack, the writer is likely to be dispensed with.

That is not the case, however, with the variation where the visual images are stills in sequence, not moving footage. It is often confusingly called an audio-visual presentation, when 'audio-visual' should cover this entire subject. It is more accurate to call it **tape/slide** (TS).

TS is often looked down on as a poor relation, but in the corporate context we are not talking about a show on the level of watching someone's holiday snaps. The photography is by professionals. The multiple projectors are programmed on, and run by, computer. And there is entirely the same synchronized sound track as a video.

TS has in addition a number of virtues which can make it the preferred choice. It could be just a question of money. While the cost of video continues to fall in real terms, TS is still a cheaper option in most circumstances. It is why video in a retailing context can have as much as half its total content as tape/slide. And why low-cost video training systems exist that are also based on stills.

Or it could be the nature of the environment for the shoot that calls for stills. That was the case in a hotel converted from an ancient country house. There the details of the building were its greatest visual selling point; and anyway the builders were still in residence, making it likely that the video camera's movement would bring something unwanted into shot.

The same increased convenience during the shoot might be suggested by low internal light levels, or night-time exteriors, or lots of individual locations. And the size of the viewing auditorium and the available projection equipment could also be deciding factors.

Most importantly, it could be for TS's particular effects. Superimposition of one image on another, or a quickly moving montage, can be made more interesting that way. Filling a wide or tall screen with single or multiple images is just as impressive as, and a good deal easier than, doing it with moving pictures.

There is therefore still no substitute – in a product launch, say, or a conference opening – for bright, clear 35 mm slides projected on to a large screen. Or for the dazzling effects of thirty or more projectors, producing (as television advertisers have found) virtual animation.

It is why there is a place for TS in the dramatic high-tech opening of the 'World of Energy' presentation at Disney's EPCOT Center in Florida. A hundred multi-sided square screens revolve singly or in batches, and have projected on to them moving images that sometimes are reminiscent of a videowall and at other times of a cinemascope screen. Yet at the end, when the script calls for butterflies, they are artwork animated in TS fashion rather than real. Because the flight and the regular beat of the wings achieves precisely the effect required – and real butterflies will not perform to order.

Not that high-tech is essential. The extraordinary 'Living Seas' pavilion is also at EPCOT. In its two-stage lead-in, an expertly photographed film is preceded by an atmospheric TS using only a handful of projectors.

And at the restored cavalry outpost of Fort Davis in Texas, a 12-minute presentation of the fort's history is easily sustained, using largely artists' impressions, by a straightforward two-projector TS.

This underlines an advantage of tape/slide. If most of your material already exists as still images – as paintings, say, or historical photographs – there are few compelling reasons for shooting them on video.

That is why Wembley chose to tell the history of the stadium by tape/slide, and why the 'Royal Britain' exhibition makes such use of it. And it is why for many years the sports track and tennis court manufacturer En Tout Cas used a fixed TS installation to explain the company's origins to visiting customers.

Equally right, for very different reasons, is the use of a wide-screen TS in the Sharks! pavilion at Sea World in Florida. After the show, the screens are lifted up – and behind them is the huge tank full of sharks. Why shoot a video when you have the real thing?

If the need arises, many varieties of tape/slide can in any case be transferred to video. Thus it has all the advantages of portability that a videotape confers, with (these days) not much loss of picture quality.

From the writer's point of view, there are two main considerations that make a tape/slide script differ from a video script. The first is that the movement has to be achieved by the use of different images rather than moving images. In part this is the director's skill in programming, but the writer, too, must think in more kaleidoscopic terms. The advantage is the possibility of using many more individual, brief images than is usual with video.

The second change is the way technologically TS achieves its effects: the interplay of the projectors, the merging and overlaying of images, the masking of slides, and so on. The use of them is again a director's skill; but understanding them is a writer's. Anyone writing tape/slide for the first time needs to make the effort to be briefed on what is involved.

The third variant is **interactive video**. It is used for point-of-sale, and language teaching is on the way; but its most important use is still training and general education. It is computer-based, and markedly different in three other respects as well.

First, the audience at any one time is usually one person. Second, that person sits with a keyboard in front of him or her as well as a screen. (Sometimes it can be a touch-screen, or a light-pen on bar codes; but the principle is the same.) The trainee interacts with the programme by using that keyboard to take decisions, select options and respond to questions. This then gives him or her feedback: analysis of the answers, or a video sequence showing what would result from a particular decision. Third, the trainee's responses determine at least partly which route he or she takes through the programme.

The interaction keeps the trainee's attention at a high level, but is not dictating the pace. Quite the reverse, since the user is in control of the speed of advance. An interactive training course can become as flexible as reading one chapter of a book at a time. Even a short course is broken into segments which allow a trainee the opportunity to take a five-minute or five-hour break.

'Hands-on' involvement is more likely to lead to the training points being retained – an important factor to set against the extra cost of interactive systems compared with normal 'linear' video. Some studies also show that total training time is reduced (as against a live course, for example), even though the measurable results are better.

Several different technological approaches to interactive video exist. In every version it is the programme designer's role which is the vital one.

All the training points, and then all the possible paths through the programme, have to be planned before any scriptwriting occurs. The designer will also be responsible for the considerable amount of computer-generated text that will appear on the screen.

The main advantage of this sort of video is that trainees can see in a realistic (but risk-free) form the consequences of an action or a decision. So the writing when it comes will mostly be dialogue scenes.

One challenge of the writer's ingenuity is producing several slightly different versions of the same scenario. This can be even more complex with two stages – the consequences of consequences – so that a multiple choice of only three at each stage produces nine different but related sequences. Not that any one trainee ever sees them all; but they still have to be written.

A less taxing approach for the writer is that of consolidation, which requires only a single scene each time. It is shown to the trainee, and the questions are put afterwards to check he or she has learned the appropriate lessons.

Interactive is just as good at instructing procedures, and such a case will as often as not use a normal voiceover. In other instances, such as teaching communication techniques, both narrative and scripted dialogue will be needed.

The closest cooperation between the programme designer and the writer is more necessary with interactive even than for other training videos, for everything that he or she writes makes sense only in the context of the complete programme. The earlier that process can begin, the better.

But then the earlier the writer is involved, the better, anyway. The reasoning behind that, and how helpful it can be, is the subject of the next chapter.

4

A Sound Basis
The fundamental importance of getting a good brief

'Please arrange your thoughts and let me know them, in their due sequence, exactly.' It was all very well for Sherlock Holmes to boss his clients about like that – they were falling over themselves to have his help. The corporate video writer is seldom in such a privileged position.

Indeed, as has been suggested earlier, there are circumstances when it can be difficult enough for a writer even to meet a client, let alone tell him to sharpen himself up.

Yet understanding the client's thinking is a basic requirement for a competent script. If a writer cannot hear that thinking expressed, or the client has not done enough thinking, the scripting process will be akin to a portrait being painted without the subject being prepared to sit for it.

The artist would not be totally at a loss in that situation. He could use photographs, and memory, and hearsay, and imagination, and the end product could well be a fine picture. But only rarely would it also be as accurate a portrayal as the subject might have wished.

His own fault, you might justifiably say. The painter and the subject should get together at the earliest possible moment. Absolutely – and just the same holds good for corporate video.

The catch with videos is the meaning of the phrase 'earliest possible'. Even defining where they *should* begin is troublesome enough. Dealing with the wildly varying points at which they actually begin demands that a writer be adaptable and quick on the uptake. (And a sense of humour does not go amiss.)

The moment of conception can be no more than a stray remark over coffee: 'A video would solve the problem.' It could simply be the Managing Director seeing someone else's, and feeling he would like one of those. It might be a sales manager looking for a more dynamic sales tool. Or the training manager seeking an effective alternative to running courses.

One thing is certain. No video writer walks in off the street and offers a script, even in the unlikely event of being able to identify where one is wanted. In all but a tiny fraction of cases, even the idea of making a video originates somewhere else, and the writer is brought in to help realize that idea.

There is therefore always something that has already happened before the writer joins the process. The question is: how much?

It is not a minor consideration. Literally anything said by any one of those directly involved is potentially of some use, and the value of hearing it unfiltered cannot be stressed too hard. Not only will the person relaying to the writer what has been said unavoidably put their own gloss on it. They may also not mention at all something which was said, but which only the writer would have noted.

The independent writer (as against the writer/producer or the in-house writer) cannot always hope to win this round. Often the initial meeting between, say, a production company and a client is exploratory, and the decision to proceed with a project will be taken later. Few companies will pay a writer to be present, or even want one there, when the business is still an unconfirmed prospect. Yet already things will be said in discussion which would be mightily helpful to hear.

The worst case I have met is for there to be two preliminary meetings. The decision is taken at the first to have a set of proposals presented at the second, after which the final go-ahead will be given. (If one of the creative ideas meets the client's approval.) Yet the writer does not attend the first meeting, and is expected to bring a choice of treatments to the second meeting. It is not a million miles away from creating bricks with straw.

Faced with that situation, it is essential for us to question and counter-question anyone we have access to, so that the feel of that first meeting – not just the bare bones minutes – can be reconstructed.

That will still be only a poor substitute for a proper brief at first hand. Fortunately, such a briefing meeting still takes place in the majority of cases.

When it is convened, any information is potentially valuable. But it is vital for certain subject areas to be included. Once again (back to the dwarfs) there are seven.

Good clients will already know the answers to the writer's questions on these subjects. The very good ones will provide the answers before the questions are asked. The less good ones will scratch their heads, and 'may need to come back to you', to come up with the answers. The bad ones will have difficulty understanding the relevance of the questions.

The seven vital headings are:

Function
Objectives
Audience
Use
Wider Context
'Political' Framework
Shelf Life

Function was looked at in some detail in the previous chapter. It is therefore only necessary here to caution once more against the job the video has to do being undermined by a subsidiary task. This means not letting training insidiously take over an internal communication video, for example, and confuse its message. The good news is that function is usually the easiest of the headings to tick off.

Objectives, however, provide the first guides to how thoroughly the client has thought through the project so far, and how much he understands the video medium.

In an ideal world, there will be a single purpose, and the client will already have identified it. In much of the real world, there will be a raft of loosely defined aims, or a long list of 'points it's essential to cover'.

The problem simply is that most clients are not video specialists. Why should they be? That is why we are there. But as a consequence, it will sometimes be necessary for an education process to begin even while the initial briefing is under way.

One producer takes a very hard line. 'If you wanted to make a corporate video to launch the Ten Commandments, I'd have to tell you to go back and reduce the number.' Even seven would be too many.

(The Ten Commandments could still be *taught*, if we used interactive video; but that would take more time than most senior people would be prepared to spend. And it is questionable whether the impact that the word 'launch' implies would be achieved by taking the interactive route.)

Fortunately we have a very persuasive reason why the client should follow our advice and re-assess what he is trying to achieve. Underlying this need to pare down the number of objectives is the single 'clipboard question' into which they must be converted if the video is to have any bite to it.

Whatever else each individual member of the audience gets from the video, they must all take away the same central idea. If they do, it is the best measure of the video's success. And a successful video is, after all, what the client is paying for.

A good example of a clear, single objective is one provided by Midland Bank for a training video. It wanted to raise its staff's awareness of the many customers who were still frightened, made nervous or over-awed by banks and bankers.

Among the secondary objectives should be ensuring that the script will be making the best use of the strengths of the medium. Where can we take the audience that they cannot otherwise go? What can we show that takes advantage of the opportunity for moving pictures?

Discussion under this heading should also cover a more subtle matter, the tone of the production. This is becoming increasingly important, with so many fields of human endeavour producing videos in abundance, to help each one maintain its own identity.

It may be the visual impression it leaves. The Savoy Hotel, for example, specified clean transitions from sequence to sequence, with none of the electronic wizardry so easily inserted in the editing phase. It was an approach very much in keeping with the idea running through the video, that quality needs no gimmicks.

It might be the overall flavour of the video. Holiday Inns were keen on three successive occasions that a strong vein of humour should run through the production.

In a training case, this will be the point at which the sense of theme and consistent style for the whole programme will begin to develop.

Get the objective fixed, precise and succinct, and we are starting to move in the right direction.

Next on the list is **audience**. To say a video should be written with its target audience in mind is to invite ridicule for stating the supremely obvious. But the significance of that statement to a writer is that he or she is most unlikely to be a member of that audience.

A supermarket video can be aimed at 'the girls at the checkout'. A hotel video might seek to influence corporate conference buyers. A health video about the benefits of breast feeding is aimed at nursing mothers. In these and hundreds of other instances, writers have consciously to think their way into the heads and emotions of people they are not.

(Even, ironically, in the breast-feeding example. It was inevitable that a woman writer was commissioned for that project; but it turned out she had never had children. Indeed, that same busy and well-qualified writer has never actually written a script which fell within the range of her previous specialist or personal experience.)

So who the audience is as a group, and who they are as individuals, is only the departure point. It is the implications of the answers to those questions that will affect the script.

What is their specialist or technical knowledge? It is dangerous to talk down to people, and useless to talk over their heads.

What do they know already? It is a complete waste of time telling them something of which they are aware, or showing them what they have seen before.

In verbal presentation training there is a guideline that you should never under-estimate your audience's intelligence, but never over-estimate their knowledge. The first half of that statement holds good for videos, too. But the second half bears refining. We want whenever we can to be more accurate than just an estimate.

What is their grasp of jargon? It is natural for the client to think and talk in the shorthand of his day-to-day life. Any video going outside the organization, however, will need to be written in plainer terms.

Where are they? It is very easy for a video to become

oriented towards the place where it is briefed. An organization may be national, but if its head office is in London or Paris or New York, the impression may seep into the video that there is little of importance beyond the metropolis.

This gives rise to two possible hazards. First, we could use visual images that are not recognized as readily in some parts of the country as in others. So the value of the pictures is reduced. Second, we may foster the antagonism that often exists when a region feels it is looked down on. So the video loses credibility.

What are their expectations? Corporate video is factual. So the audience expects to be informed. They also quite enjoy being surprised by learning something they did not know.

(The client may easily be too close to a subject to realize its significance in this respect. The Savoy Hotel, for example, saw nothing remarkable in the fact that it manufactured its own beds. It had done so for years. But how many other hotels do the same? To the audience, it was unusual, and therefore interesting, and therefore memorable. And it served to support the central thesis that no detail is too small in a top-quality hotel.)

In addition, because of their domestic television experience, the audience expects production quality. They do not expect – or at least do not want – to be bored, irritated, confused or preached at.

The worthier the subject, the more important the last of those turn-offs becomes. A major brewing company concerned about alcoholism among its publicans was not going to get very far with just a sombre on-screen presenter detailing depressing statistics. The writer must be looking for ways to make an uncomfortable or pedestrian message more palatable.

Do they hold any opposing views to the ones being put forward in the video? The consensus among video-makers would probably be that you should never introduce negatives, and there are good reasons for that. But there will still be occasions when it is necessary to address an alternative or a prejudice head-on, even if the manner of dealing with it remains positive. Certainly the writer should find out all the attitudes that prevail on the subject in hand, even if they do not all find their way into the script.

Is English their native language – or just a common denominator? When English is used as the communication medium between different nationalities, as it often is in multi-national organizations, international trade, politics and tourism, the writer needs to exercise even more care in choosing words. The fact that the listener cannot turn back the page and read it again to check its meaning is more relevant than ever. And even the English and the Americans are, as Oscar Wilde rather tartly observed, divided by a common language.

There is also the cultural barrier that is erected by the presence of more than one nationality in the audience. If someone from London will not necessarily recognize buildings in Manchester, England, there is even less chance of their doing so if they are shown Manchester, New Hampshire, or Kansas or Georgia, or any of the other Manchesters in the United States.

Cultural implications stretch further. As someone who likes to use a historical strand in a script given half an opportunity, I have to be extremely choosy about the material if there is a multi-national audience. But the list of tripwires stretches through the arts to driving habits, from religion to cooking.

How old are they? The creative treatment may well need to reflect a low or a high average age. Just as marketing increasingly looks at segments within its total market, and often treats them differently, a video may need to do just the same.

Are they single-sex or mixed? Even the most emancipated are willing to admit there are differences between men and women. When it comes to looking for creative ideas, this can matter very much, even if we are forced to generalize a little.

Few men or women take much interest in the fashions of the opposite sex, for example. The attraction of games such as football and cricket has passed most women by. The finer points of patchwork and crocheting will leave most men cold.

It is not a case of giving in to sexual stereotypes. It is simply the risk of irritating or boring half the audience that we want to be aware of, and to avoid.

The emphasis of all this ferreting out of information about the audience has been on the writer. But actually the client is just as likely to be unrepresentative of the people who will see the video. This is in addition to being too close to the subject, as in the hotel bed example above.

This is usually more of a pain in the neck when it comes to the judgements made on a completed script. But what we want at the briefing is (at worst) beliefs, and (at best) validated research. If we suspect we are being fed assumptions, guesses or prejudices, we need to probe a little further.

The **use** of the video, the circumstances in which it will be seen, will influence both the flavour and aspects of the structure. It could even require one of the variations in format, such as a videowall or tape/slide, discussed in the previous chapter.

Rarely is a video intended to stand truly alone. Not the least reason is that the successful video prompts reactions or questions with which only a human being can deal. Even an attention-grabbing videowall is meant to attract passers-by to the exhibition stand. But there can be big differences between the need to tell a rounded story and other videos in integrated or springboard roles.

The rounded story is not merely one with a beginning, middle and end – they all have that. (Or should have.) The rounded story is one that takes the audience through a full narrative, however brief, so that any subsequent discussion is prompted from within it. Like a brochure, it can thus be seen independently if need be. Many marketing, internal communication and educational videos are rounded in this way.

Integrated use is video in product launch or interactive guise, where individual elements only make complete sense when put together with all the others – and yet they have to be written individually. Tape/slide is commonly used in product launches or conferences in just this way, as a prelude to a live speaker, who will also be supported by slides.

The springboard role is typically a training one. The video is intended to stimulate the subsequent trainer-led discussion. Often the training points will be in the video, to allow the trainer to refer back to them, but deliberately unemphasized. That allows the 'did you notice...' type of discussion.

Sometimes the video will be structured in two halves, a 'before' and 'after' or cause and effect, with the discussion in between.

The place in which the video will be used can also be an influence. Normally the audience will see it on a standard television set. But use a theatre, cinema or conference centre, and the director may seek to create effects in other ways.

Investigating the **wider picture** makes sure both that the video is used to its best advantage, and also that the writer does not waste time.

The fact that, in a training context, a video will usually only be part of a comprehensive programme has already been touched on. But all forms of video seldom exist in a vacuum. So we need to ask:

Has anything preceded the video? This could have taken many forms, but the most dangerous is an earlier video. Good or bad, that previous video adopted a creative approach which it is essential to be aware of, and probably desirable to avoid.

Is there to be any supporting material? This is normal in training or induction, and common in education; but it often applies to marketing as well. A brochure, for example, might be produced in tandem with the video.

The alignment of this 'book of the film' with the video is primarily the producer's job. But if – as should happen – most of the visual images in both print and video are the same, it could affect the script. (It would certainly affect the shoot, if a stills photographer is to be there at the same time.) Perhaps artwork or graphics already exist, that could be incorporated.

Is anything complementary happening? In any sizeable organization, profit-making or not, a video is not likely to be the sole weapon being deployed. Publicity posters, an advertising campaign and leaflets are all possibilities which the client may not appreciate should form part of the video brief. But if they can, all those need to run in harness. Even if some already exist, the video should at least run in parellel with them. Commonality of themes and ideas between them strengthens each by association with the others.

One bullet is all well and good. Several have to be better.

What has already been done elsewhere? In most business cases, the client will know better than you what his competitors have produced, because it is his job. Finding that out saves coming up with a brilliant idea that has already been used. It does not stop it being brilliant, but it will probably stop it being in the script. We have better things to do with our time than re-invent the wheel.

The **'political' framework** can be a substantial snare for the unwary. Most writers work on their own. They may, therefore, be blissfully ignorant of the power plays, the vested interests and the personality clashes from which every organization suffers to some extent. These would not matter a jot, were it not for the fact that they loom much larger after the script has been written. The organization's snipers, sceptics and professional point-scorers gather like the vultures that shadow travellers lost in the desert.

So, to prevent multiple passes at the script as they all tear little bits off it – six drafts is the worst case I have so far met – try to establish at this early stage: What must be said? What must not be said? Who or what must be shown? Who or what must not be shown? What is likely to change soon? (Organization structures and ownership of subsidiaries are sometimes much more fluid than an innocent outsider would think possible.) What is the corporate culture that the video must reflect? And perhaps most importantly, who is not at the briefing whose input might be critical – and therefore better taken sooner rather than later?

Compared with some of its heavyweight compatriots, the last of the seven, **shelf life**, is a more straightforward business. Short-term internal communications or training may only last a matter of months. Marketing videos may be needed for up to two years, induction for three. Generic training products such as those of Video Arts and Rank may last ten years.

Some of the implications of the decision on shelf-life are down to the director. Fashions in clothes, for example, can date notoriously quickly. But so do other things. Company results, market share percentages, logos, models of cars and their number plates, the names of people in particular jobs and the exact titles of those jobs are among them. All these and more fall within the writer's sphere, because they can be scripted either in or out.

Shelf life is another good reason for avoiding talking heads. It is bad enough showing an individual at work who then leaves (or, worse still, is sacked). The video is fatally wounded if someone talking to camera, with all the emphasis that implies, moves on to pastures new.

We should not make ourselves hostages to fortune. It may not be common to be faced with the Head of Personnel recording his words of welcome for the induction video, and three days later dropping dead. But it happened. And the equivalent disruption can easily do so again.

In that particular instance, the new suddenly promoted Head of Personnel had other things than a video on his mind, and the entire project was shelved.

So if in doubt, script out. You will not lose many friends that way. Shelf life has a habit of ending up much longer than expected. I recently learned of a marketing video still being used five years after I had written it.

There are some important items not included in the list of seven. That is a deliberate omission rather than an oversight. It is because, while relevant, the others do not affect the writer in quite the same way, and sometimes are negligible in their impact on the script.

The most obvious absentee, perhaps, is **length**. One of the most difficult questions that a client can put is how long the video will be, or even should be. The answer that it will be as long as it needs to be is apparently facetious. But in fact it is often the most honest assessment that can made at an early stage.

Length is a product of use, objectives and content, and the first of those will commonly dominate, especially when considering the minimum end of the scale. Videos in integrated or springboard format could be as short as 3 minutes, and I have met one of 60 seconds. A computer launch made up of nine linked modules ran for a total of only 45 minutes.

A rounded story is unlikely to be able to say all it wants to in less than that average of 5 minutes, but in some cases it might not need much more.

Maximum length is just as variable. The need to keep visitors moving in a museum could set a limit of 3 minutes on a self-operated display. Yet even leaving aside interactive (which by its nature is never seen continuously from start to finish, and is as likely to be constrained by disc capacity as anything else), training and education videos could well run to 20 or 30 minutes. This is particularly true if the video is intended to be seen in sections, or if it has a dramatized storyline, as many generic training videos do.

But we should be sensitive to the willingness of an audience to sit for that length of time and maintain the high level of attention that we want. Fifteen minutes is a reasonable rule of thumb for an upper limit, even when discussion follows immediately. Certainly anything running longer than that needs to be looked at with care to see if it needs cutting.

For we definitely do not automatically get more effect from greater length. The construction company defending itself against despoiling the environment overstated its case in a 32-minute video. The financial services company that produced a 38-minute induction video would have got as much value for the money it spent by keeping it under the mattress.

Much longer educational videos for use in the home or at school do not disprove the rule, for they are obviously exceptions.

For example, the BBC's excellent natural history *Life on Earth* is a slimmed-down version of a television series, even at 150 minutes. It lends itself to being dipped into at almost any point. And *St Paul's: the Story of a Great Cathedral* is a leisurely (52 minutes) and atmospheric documentary that would also not be out of place on television.

Both in any case still adhere to length being a product of use, objectives and content,

So, given that length is not defined (by a specified slot in a programme, say, or assessed by the producer already), a good starting point for answering the client is how much it is possible to get into 10 minutes. It is no accident that very many rounded story videos – marketing, induction, education, even training – end up between 8 and 12 minutes.

Of course, a client may specify a length. Unless I already know the client very well, however, I start by treating that figure with a considerable pinch of salt. The last time a client dictated a length, the finished video overshot it by 50% – because of all the extra material the client insisted had to be included.

If the **budget** has taken a long time to make its formal appearance here, it is simply because the writer is so rarely involved in its compilation (unless also wearing the hat of producer/director). Indeed, the figure itself is irrelevant to the script. What matters is the proportion allocated to the shooting of the script. And that matters a good deal.

If the star of your cinema epic is already being paid $5 million, the difference between three extras or four in a scene will scarcely ripple the budgetary pond. Corporate video is effectively never like that.

The budget is often too slim for comfort and always limiting in some degree. Investment (as in films and, to a lesser extent, television) in the hope of later profit is very much the exception. The cost has usually to be justified internally for its own sake, and the intangible returns do not impress the financially cautious. The result will often be not only a fixed but a tight budget.

So, as before, it is the implications of the decisions that concern us as writers. If the Gleneagles Hotel is owed favours by an air-taxi company and a car-hire firm, by all means write in a helicopter shot of a Rolls-Royce driving through the glens. If the armed services can turn a training flight into a photographic one, fine – plan for some extravagant visuals.

But in most circumstances, imagination has to be tempered with realism, and the producer's lead followed. You must expect to be 'given the creative parameters', as one producer put it.

There are four main factors that, while not necessarily critical, can influence cost in ways the writer needs to bear in mind.

First, how straightforward are the locations? Only in high-budget cases will one or more sets, with all their attendant costs, be built in a studio especially for one video. But using real offices or real streets is still only half the problem solved. The crew (and, if necessary, the actors) have to get to each place and set up. More time can easily be taken up, and money spent, on travelling to and fro than on filming. In extreme cases, where locations are at opposite ends of the country, or in different countries, this can get out of hand. We must be certain we need every location we propose to use.

Second, are actors being used; and if so, is there lip-synchronized dialogue? The number of actors has a direct financial impact: they are all being paid, even when they are not in front of the camera. So avoid one-line walk-on parts and epic crowd scenes. Lip-synchronized dialogue is slow to film, anyway. Complex scenes with lots of characters interacting are slower still.

Third, are there any special props – and if so, what are the ramifications of them? The food being eaten has to be fresh whenever it is shot. Fairly easy if it is a salad, more tricky if it is a soufflé. Into this category, too, come effects, such as dry ice, special vehicles (such as a police car or a fire engine), weaponry, blood, floods and broken glass. Different again, but also not cheap, are computer graphics. Enthusiasm for the dramatic may need to be toned down to the realistic.

Lastly, how complicated is the editing? Post-production is a big item in any budget. While the writer need not get over-excited about it, we may have to discuss with the director the practicability of something we want to script before we commit it to paper.

Whether writer or director, there is only one safe time to breach the previously agreed budgetary restraints. That is when the client insists on adding something, or making a change, which cannot be done without additional cost. And only then when the full extent of the cost has been made clear to him.

For example, a script signed off by the client was recorded by a top-notch voiceover artist. Only on hearing the finished product was the client aware of, and unhappy with, a double meaning in the words. 'Members of the fourth generation of the family are still active in the company' was intended to carry the message of continuity of family involvement. It suddenly seemed as if they were all geriatrics, when in fact they were all under forty. The line had to be changed to 'Many fourth-generation members of the family are now active in the company', and the voicover re-booked to re-record half a page of script.

Because the client was a gentleman and a believer in the best possible quality, he paid without demur. They are not always so professional in their attitude.

Casting is another area in which the writer is unlikely to become involved. On rare occasions, part of the planning will include the use of a particular named actor or actress. But the script will only be specifically written with them in mind if it is following a recognizable format – usually a television series – and in that case probably the original writers will be employed.

The same will apply when a television personality or comedian appears in front of the camera. Writers who know their personal style and have written for them already will be brought in.

The writer will have equally little say in the selection of the voiceover. The director will have more knowledge of who is suitable for which type of subject matter, and often will present several cassettes to the client so he can give an opinion. The writer may not even know until the script is delivered whether the voiceover is to be male or female.

That is not necessarily a bad thing. The text should be driven by the content and the objectives, not by who is going to be speaking the words. If the script is competent, it can be spoken by anyone whose business is to speak scripts.

The final heading not yet mentioned is **timescale**. The lucky writer is asked how long the script will take. The less lucky will be told when it has to be delivered.

In practice it is rare for the timescale to be completely ludicrous – but there is often pressure. A great deal has to happen after the script is agreed, and most of it takes a lot longer than writing a script. If the video is ever to appear at all, the critical first stage – agreeing the script – must not drag on.

But even 24 hours, the shortest time I have ever had for a first draft, was tiring and stressful but not – in the peculiar circumstances – unrealistic. Ten days should be ample when no unusual research is involved. Longer than that is a luxury.

Those are figures based on experience with the 'standard' corporate video, the 10-12-minute rounded story. A full dramatization, an interactive programme or a sequence of integrated scripts will naturally take considerably longer.

There is not a lot of advantage, however, in having too much time. The script will definitely be tuned and chamfered and polished, if not more radically changed, and that process will be the result of inputs other than the writer's. The sooner we deliver, the sooner the revisions can be incorporated and the script signed off. Delaying that moment is in nobody's interest.

Literally anything that is said at the brief, by anyone, is worth listening to. Although crucial points may be immediately obvious, it is rare to be able to judge so readily that something is useless, which is the only good reason for ignoring it.

In most corporate circumstances, however, the writer is having to move up a steep learning curve during that first meeting, and everything that is said will add up to a great deal. So it is not the ideal moment to think about the script. It is a time for understanding rather than analysis, for questions and answers rather than creative proposals.

Therefore most of what is said is worth recording as well as listening to, so that it can be reflected on later, in a less demanding environment.

Particularly helpful to note down are the actual words a client uses to make a point or describe a situation. Nine times out of ten I find that the script can make use of one or more such statements.

This is not, as it might appear, a recipe for getting the client to write the script. It is simply drawing on the strengths of all involved. The client knows more about the subject than we do, and is likely to express what he says in a way that the organization finds acceptable. He expresses it, moreover, in spoken words, of which the script must consist.

It is only a particular example of the all-embracing one: paying attention to and making a note of everything, in case it should prove useful.

How the writer manages to capture all this information is, to an extent, a personal matter. I am not a great fan of miniature tape recorders, because of the tedium and loss of time transcribing the tape afterwards. And it would have to be transcribed, since I find it essential to work from notes that I can spread in front of me and cross-reference.

The order in which items appear in the script could be wildly at odds with the order they are briefed. I would not like to sacrifice being able to flip back and forth between them as I write.

Tape recorders are also easily overwhelmed when two people talk at once or overlap. So I will always take copious old-fashioned notes, and ask to recap if someone's speech runs ahead of my writing. Later on, I would prefer to have too much than too little when I am sitting on my own assembling the script.

The same principle informs my willingness to take whatever the client has to offer, subject only to the physical problem of removing trunkloads of literature. Brochures and other promotional material, internal reports, market sector surveys, history books: all have potentially a part to play.

They may simply help us up that learning curve. But they can also be sources of the correct jargon, of factual support for otherwise bland statements, even of direct quotations.

The question 'Would this be useful at all?' is thus one I welcome. Three times out of four the answer will be yes.

In the same spirit, I am always keen to hear other people's first reactions. Given the classic trio of writer, director and producer, it is inconceivable that the other two will sit at the briefing with minds in neutral while the writer does all the work.

At the very least, therefore, a review afterwards of what the others in the video team think will consolidate a writer's impressions. Better still if they stimulate a train of thought that has not yet occurred to us. Best of all if they provide keys to the subsequent structuring of the script. Even a consensus against taking a particular creative line will save time and effort pursuing it.

The writer, after all, does not necessarily have a monopoly of listening skills and ideas. If anyone deserves to have the accusation of professional arrogance levelled at them, let it not be us.

One nagging thought remains. Have we understood not only what the client said but what he really needs?

It is essential to take away from the briefing what lies at the heart of the video project – the *ultimate* objective. And while it is not necessary to agree with the producer who says he will 'challenge everything – to see how strongly the convictions are held', experience suggests that the client's thinking will often be refined during the process of briefing his requirements.

Exposure to increasing amounts of television and ever greater quantities of video have created in many clients a false sense of how easy it must be to do, because so many people are doing it. They can therefore be genuinely surprised at what is expected of them – of how much thinking has to be done before a script can be written.

If that reads like a plea to clients to be as rigorous and analytical with their preparation for a video as they would be for a set of annual accounts or a rights issue, it is. The significance for the writer is that we have to help the client to that state of grace if he has not identified the need for it by the time the project is being briefed.

When we come to writing the script, it should not be merely a means of re-defining the video's aims. What we should be doing is creating a vehicle that will satisfy those aims in the most effective way.

With a solid briefing behind us, covering all the ground suggested in this chapter, that is the point we have now reached.

5

The Creative Idea
Finding ways to present the subject matter

Aviators are not famous for their modesty. Thus it is that there are, among the snappy sayings of which as a breed they are fond, many which laud their own ability. One of the more popular is that any fool can get an aircraft off the ground, but it takes a pilot to get it back down again.

Although I am a former pilot myself (and naturally the exception to the rule about modesty), I have never understood the logic of that particular aphorism. The take-off phase of a flight requires different skills to those of landing, but just as many of them; and if important switches or controls have been overlooked, take-off is not the perfect time to find out. It is not coincidence that in airliners you are encouraged to fasten your safety belt for take-off as well as for landing.

It would be much more accurate, if less deft, to say that any fool can keep an aircraft flying once it is in the air. It takes a pilot to get it there and bring it back.

In that form it is an idea directly equivalent to writing a corporate video. There is always a section in the middle of a video which, as one cynical producer said, 'even the client can write'. That may not in fact be literally true; but in principle the factual content the video has to put across does require the least skill. The most creative bit is the getting there, and the getting back.

But not in fact the only creative bit. The first challenge that the writer must surmount is the provision of a plausible, consistent and watchable framework for the detailed content.

'Plausible' underlines the need to remain credible. The audience must be able to believe it, or else they will switch off, mentally if not physically. In a marketing case, for example, that includes not making unbelievable or unprovable claims. In a training video, it means not showing people so flawless that they seem to be destined for canonization.

'Consistent' emphasizes the single message at which our rifle medium is best. To change the metaphor, everything must hang together. A single thread must run through it all.

'Watchable' reminds us that the predictable, the pedestrian, the pretentious and the placid all work against us. The dynamic, the original, the unexpected and the thought-provoking all work for us.

The framework does not have to be complicated. There are many instances when a straightforward approach is the best. If we are extolling the virtues of a hotel or a city or a country, we know we will need to deal with where it is and its facilities and what makes it special. If we are talking about an organization, we will have to be concerned with what it does, and how and where it does it.

The order in which we deal with the items, however, is where we start to impose ourselves on the raw material. Even if a guest goes in through the lobby of a hotel first and then to a bedroom and then to a restaurant, there is absolutely no reason for the video to do the same. Checking in is uninspiring; bedrooms in all but the grandest hotels are more alike than different. So sandwich them, if they are to appear at all, between more interesting items.

Take the case of a video for the Gleneagles Hotel. The order was: location; origin of the building; the standards they believe in; the range of the facilities within the hotel; how easily it could be reached; the golf; the other leisure facilities; and the hotel as a base for travel within Scotland. The restaurants only got two quick shots, the bedrooms one.

In terms of the thread, location appears in three different forms – because that was what was being underlined. As the script said explicitly: 'Truly great hotels are known by where they are as well as what they are'.

It is an example of what a producer called 'repeated blows on the same nail' – with the nail being his interpretation of the single message. The writer's skill, he felt, was 'hammering it in many ways without the audience noticing'.

The emphasis we place on a particular point is another way to strengthen the message. Consider the video for a manufacturer of sports equipment and surfaces such as tennis courts and running tracks. It could have concentrated on the technical, and been pretty boring to most audiences. It could have dwelt on its tennis origins – but that would have had elitist overtones that the company wished to avoid when selling to egalitarian local councils. Instead it focused on the way its wide range of products had become part of everyone's life. 'As part of our wish to see sport available ever more widely, we produce equipment to suit every pocket and every possibility...'

The items we select for the script will also shape it. Show the fact, as was mentioned earlier in the book, that the Savoy Hotel makes rather than buys its beds, because that is highly unusual. But ignore the fact that it bakes its own bread, because every self-respecting establishment should do that.

We can also look to group items together. The Philippines has a natural four-way geographical split (north, centre, south and Manila), and the client pointed it out to us. (Because, being a good client, she had done her thinking before the brief started.)

Plymouth had no such obvious divisions. But using the idea of places in and around Plymouth where work and leisure exist side by side helped to provide a different slant for the framework.

Whatever we do, we must keep that central theme running through the script. The enormous variety of activities within the Café Royal was hung on the thread of a day in its life, compared to the world outside its doors. 'So when London takes time off for lunch, the Café Royal stays at work – providing lunch...'

The linkage through the Philippines video was provided by dance. All the geographical areas have major cultural differences as well, which are reflected in their local dance forms. There was also the extra benefit of dance being visually attractive, and unusual to the intended European audience.

For, however straightforward the content of this core section of the video, its visual aspect remains as important as ever. We must not lose sight of those characteristics we established at the outset. Let the pictures do all they can, and make them move.

Visual, too, was the idea 'More than meets the eye' that ran through a video about Birmingham. The phrase kept appearing in unexpected places, like the headline of a passer-by's newspaper.

Often, though, the straightforward approach is not appropriate. The subject matter may be too mundane or too familiar. In a training case, it could be too unpalatable. After all, who likes being told what they are doing wrong, and would they please improve?

In such cases, a more imaginative structure is needed. We are looking for a treatment that does not lose the message, but is more likely to hold the audience's attention.

There is no surefire formula, but some very different examples show the sort of thinking needed.

A video for the ground services side of an airline was concerned, as service industries so often are, with improving behaviour towards customers. The objective was to get people like baggage handlers, check-in staff and caterers to recognize that their actions mattered. The framework adopted had echoes of the game of Cluedo. The different parts of the airport were the rooms of the house, and customers disappeared whenever they were treated with indifference or just plain badly. The message, quite simply, was that customers driven away by bad service are never seen by the airline again.

As part of the overall style, too, the airport was portrayed as frightening – as indeed it can be for many irregular passengers, but never is for people who work there every day.

Another training video, this time for a hotel group, moved on to a parallel track to make its point. The objective here was to cut down wasted expenditure in areas like heat, light, breakages and laundry. The scenario put a thoughtless and careless visitor into a private house, doing all the things the client told us hotel staff do, and causing his hosts untold heartache. As he was finally leaving, the script said:

	Now no doubt you'll say this whole story has been exaggerated. No-one would really waste money like that. Least of all anyone like you. Would you?
Examples in which a very short reprise of the guest's action is pulled through to a comparable wasteful action in a hotel. Each hotel action finishes with a freeze	

frame and the sound of old-style
till:
Man leaves door open/Hotel front
door open. Camera reveals it is
wedged open.
Dishwasher ....

And the video was doing one of the things it does best. The smashing of plates and glasses and the spillage on tablecloths had to be staged only once.

Another example comes from information technology, which is a notoriously difficult field to deal with. Computers are visually not much more interesting than cardboard boxes, and the problems they solve frequently do not lend themselves to straightforward visual treatment.

A particularly powerful but compact mainframe was launched by ICL at a time when separate data-processing solutions had proliferated, even within the same organization. To make sense of the computer's selling point – it could do all the jobs currently being done by different computers dotted around a company – it was necessary to understand the drawbacks of the current situation.

The approach adopted was to mark out on a studio floor a symbolic structure for an organization. Departments were vertical, the layers within each department horizontal. The voiceover then talked of 'introducing all the benefits of computers'. Representative computers – in fact anonymous desk-top terminals – were placed all over the organization for various roles. But at the same time, walls began to grow along the lines of the departmental segments, gradually isolating each computer from the others. The script went on:

> To make sure no part of the organization works in isolation, and information is shared properly, we have to ensure that we can communicate it.

Man starts to lay broad green tapes
to connect up one computer to
another. As he does so, the dividing
walls continue to grow differentially,
some of them now high enough to impede

his progress and make communication more difficult	...up and down in each department... ...laterally at each level...
By now the job of laying tapes is getting quite difficult	...and diagonally wherever it's needed to get the job done better.
He is now in one of the department segments with walls so high it looks like a street. There is a confusion of green tapes going in all directions above his head.	

The technical problem of connecting up a battery of different computers had been made visual.

And, again, the video used one of the medium's strengths. The same idea could also have been explained in a brochure; but the movement, the threat of the growing walls and the increasing tangle of tapes created much greater impact.

A different approach altogether was adopted by Holiday Inns in Canada. Here location was the key message, but location of all the hotels: wherever you are, you are never far from a Holiday Inn.

Simply to fill a map of Canada with place names was a job far better suited to a brochure. So the thread was to pick out highlights of Canadian history and suggest, in a none too serious way, that each event took the course it did because of the lack of Holiday Inns. For example:

St Lawrence river	In 1759, the English general Wolfe was on a tour of the St Lawrence. His trip ended in disappointment on the Heights of
Quebec, early print	Abraham in Quebec. *Wolfe:* 'I climb all this way on what
Portrait of General Wolfe	I might say is a very badly maintained path, and then there isn't even anywhere to stay.' *Voiceover:* It was enough to make anyone expire.
Death of Wolfe	So he did.
Introduce picture of Downtown	Pity.
Quebec Holiday Inn	He was only a few years early.

One effective route to take, if the material allows, is telling a story. A Royal Navy PR film needed to show all the various sub-units within the Navy, but a documentary format tends towards the plodding shopping list: 'There is also the Royal Maritime Auxiliary Service.' It is far more watchable to follow reactions to an unfolding threat across, say, a week, and show each of the many arms of the service contributing to its war readiness.

Generic training videos (those made by production houses for multiple sale, in both linear and interactive form) use the same approach. Take one or more business situations, or a typical company, and follow through the action, drawing conclusions from it.

However large an imaginary company, or a real one, come to that, the settings portrayed remain small-scale. Most people, after all, only work in units of a few people at any one time, and that should be what the trainee sees.

Or we can follow the interaction of one static central character, in a bar or a shop, with a succession of diffcrent customers.

Inherently uninteresting products (at least for showing on video) need a little bit of lateral thinking, too. Instead of the product, concentrate on the process of manufacturing it. Or place emphasis on what the product does rather than what it is. (An approach I found it helpful to apply to extruded polyurethane and children's rusks.) Or, with subjects heavy on detail, like insurance procedures and managing filing systems, leaven the bread by showing the results of correct or incorrect actions rather than just how to do it.

Whether the idea for the central portion of a video is straightforward or not, it is a simple matter to introduce once that approach has been decided. The structure so far, therefore, looks like this:

```
┌──────────┐
│ Introduce│
│ subject  │
└────┬─────┘
     │
┌────┴─────┐
│ Detailed │
├──────────┤
│   case   │
├──────────┤
│    in    │
├──────────┤
│ segments │
└──────────┘
```

As was outlined earlier, however, this is the aircraft already in flight. We still have to get up in the air.

We are faced here once again with audience expectations. It can even be audience apathy. The average person watches hours of television a week, at quite a low level of attention most of the time. Sometimes they are just slumped in front of the set. Why should those well-established habits be altered for another 10 minutes' viewing?

In addition, only those who have been journeying to the centre of the earth for several years can fail to have been exposed to corporate videos in some form. And the number of videos is rapidly increasing.

Even willing members of the audience, therefore, may be jaded, and put off by the thought of watching another one. Others will have their minds elsewhere, on their last telephone call or their next meeting or what they would like for lunch. Yet others will have already made up their minds about the subject of the video, and be no better than cool towards it.

All this disparate thinking needs to be brought swiftly to the point. Our point.

Taking the introduction head-on is not likely to achieve that. 'Head-on' means a picture of the building or city we are talking about as the first image, or the name of the organization as the first words.

An early classic of this unhelpful sort was pictures of a butterfly pursued across open ground by a man holding a net. The first words of the voiceover were 'This man collects butterflies'.

Even less use is a presenter talking to camera as the opening visual, *saying* the name of the building or the company. And captions on screen containing those words achieve just as little.

This last is troublesome, since many clients insist on a title. As virtually all the audience know why and what they are watching, I see no mileage in stating the obvious, such as *An XYZ Training Video or XYZ Induction*.

If forced to use a title, I would opt for something slightly more intriguing. (The hotel cost-saving video referred to earlier was just called *The Visitor*.) Or I would try to take a leaf out of the cinema's book, as some training films do, and have a sequence before the titles, and run the action on underneath them.

But if a client is dead set on something plain, it is not a battle worth fighting.

Title or not, however, what we still need is a hook.

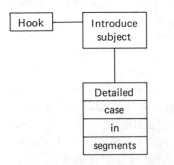

We have to have the audience's attention before they can absorb anything factual. Soften them up first, in the words of one producer. Create a window, in the expression of another, through which the message can be lodged.

There are many ways of doing that. It does not have to be extravagant to be effective. The only criterion we have to satisfy is that we do not start where the audience might expect us to.

The Savoy Hotel, despite eschewing all forms of technological gimmickry in its video, still had a hook. It opened in black and white, focused on a candelabra on a piano. Someone was playing and singing *As Time Goes By*. The focus changed, blurring the candelabra and showing the pianist beyond it. The picture changed to colour, and the camera pulled back to reveal a cocktail lounge.

Only then did the voiceover start, and only then was the location identified as the Savoy.

If budget and circumstance allow, 'wow' visuals can be used. These are pictures whose relevance is not immediately apparent, but which are sufficiently impressive in their own right to demand attention.

The Gleneagles video is one example. It opened with a Rolls-Royce being tracked by a helicopter as it was driving down a glen. Gradually the car pulled away, and the camera moved gently past it to pick up the road winding ahead of it. Then the helicopter pulled up, and the destination of the Rolls – still several miles away – was revealed as Gleneagles.

The Royal Navy, seeking to destroy the negative myths about a posting to Rosyth in Scotland, opened with airborne shots close to the distinctive girders of the Forth Rail Bridge, and then contrasted them with the soaring suspension towers of the Road Bridge.

Flying in all its forms is a gift to a video. There are few more dramatic scenes, even to the initiated, than the launch of an aircraft from a carrier. It was with 40 seconds of such powerful pictures that a video for GEC Avionics hooked its audience. The voiceover, when it came, had only to point out that all aircraft now depend on avionics, and that the common factor between all these examples was the company's products. ('Wow' visuals, if not used at the beginning, have a place in the central portion as well. But there they are employed to make the detailed case more memorable.)

A different use of visuals is to tease with them. It is not clear at first what the pictures represent, although in fact they are genuinely to do with the subject. Or there is no obvious link between the pictures and the subject. Or there is no apparent connection between each of several visuals. Or there is a contrast between the visuals and the sounds. The opening of the Philippines video referred to in Chapter 2 is an example of this technique.

It is no accident that all of these not only use visuals, but use them first. Let the pictures do all they can.

Sometimes the hook is sufficiently complex, or far enough away from the subject ('coming in from the side', as it is called), for an extra element to be needed. This is the bridge:

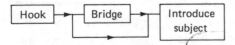

A brilliantly creative hook is worthless if a bridge cannot be built from it to the subject.

A British Airways video was concerned with getting staff to keep thinking competitively, not to rest on their laurels. It opened in a swimming pool. Beautifully lit, and shot much of the time in slow motion, the pictures showed a man – one of only three people present – preparing to make a dive.

It was not until the man was slowly climbing up the ladder to the top board that the voiceover made the bridge. 'It's been a long hard climb so far.' It went on to suggest that, however good you are, you will still only be judged on today's performance. Just like the diver.

A very different video, handling the unlikely task of deflecting criticism (on health and nutrition grounds) of the sausage, had a similarly surprising hook and bridge. It opened with a man in a suburban street clearly on some sort of clandestine errand. He eventually reaches what looks like a public lavatory below ground level. Money changes hands with someone unseen, a package is handed up to him and he scurries away as a police siren is heard in the distance.

Back inside his home, weary but relieved to be safe, he opens the package. It contains sausages. The bridge was made by the voiceover asking if we really wanted to make sausages as difficult to obtain as this.

The limits to creativity here are only the imagination of the writer, the necessity of bridging back to the subject and the client's willingness to accept what he may regard as a too unconventional approach.

Comparison is one method. We take professionalism for granted in other jobs – why not in this one? (For a cleaning company.) Each field has its own specialists – so does this one. (For a conference organizer.)

Analogy is very similar. Some animals evolved, others did not survive – it's the same with companies. (For a training film encouraging greater adaptability among employees.) Different colours combine to produce strong white light. It's the same if you put companies together – you get something stronger. (For a company marketing a new image as one entity instead of three separate companies.)

This route is useful with difficult subjects. What sort of hook, I was asked on a course, could demonstrate the nature of AIDS? Some show-stopping visual is clearly needed. The terrifying armies of tropical ants that inexorably devour all in their path seem to me to be analogous to the way in which the body's immune system is destroyed.

Even the much more restricted framework of interactive video can still use analogy. A programme about budgeting started with a car being driven. 'Budgeting is like that – bringing lots of different activities together at the same time.'

History is a rich source of hooks that will bridge comfortably into different subjects, even leaving aside the obvious historical connections that companies, cities and countries already have built into them.

For example, an internal conference for the Post Office was much concerned with planning. It used an integrated video about the Duke of Marlborough. While his military skill won the battles, his administrative flair paved the way for success. For nearly two months before the Battle of Blenheim:

Blenheim on map	He had been making arrangements that would allow him to carry out his main plan.
German castle	Permission to pass through the lands of different German princes
Old-fashioned bridge	Bridges in good repair
Food at an old inn or farm	Provisions ready
Early bank	Credit arranged at banks
Close up on soldiers' feet	Even new boots waiting for his army along the route of his advance
Merge into business group at planning meeting	
	It's just the sort of multi-layered planning that we're familiar with in business
	Or at least we ought to be....

One other example of hooking and bridging – this time about a building. Whitbread's 200-year-old brewery in London was taken out of commission, re-furbished and then re-opened as a conference centre, The Brewery. The script of the video to market it in its new role opened this way:

Sounds of simple building work	
Early building work in progress	
	Kings and dreamers like to leave their mark on the sands of time
Old buildings on way to completion	

Pyramid
Forbidden City, Peking
Acropolis   We who come after them
                                             can only marvel at their
Taj Mahal   rich legacy to us
Neuschwanstein
Statue of Liberty
French chateau   But for practical men and women,
                                             buildings – however long they
Early, modest church   last – have a job of work to
                                             do
Old residential building still
in use
Old shopfront still in use
'George' Inn, Southwark
Introduce Whitbread name using
'George' sign   The first Samuel Whitbread
Reynolds portrait of Whitbread   was a practical man.
                                             And the job of work his building had
                                             to do was
Early brewing   brew beer.
                                             The brewery was in Chiswell Street,
Map of London showing Chiswell   London
Street......

There remains the matter of landing the aircraft. If the first
thing the audience sees and hears is important, because it should
encourage them to keep watching, the last thing they see and hear
is vital, because it is what they are most likely to remember. It is
the place, therefore, where we stand the most chance of our
message being heard and retained.

This is where that single clipboard question comes into its own.
Once we have that, we can write a few, compact statements to
encapsulate it.

In the hotel costs case, it was short and sharp: 'Let's get our
controllable costs under control.'

In the Café Royal case:

   Matchless service with a personal
   touch –
   right in the heart of London –

right through the day –
every day of the year.

In The Brewery case:

Samuel Whitbread, as an honest and forward-
looking brewer, had little in common with
kings and dreamers

But he, too, left his mark

The Brewery

A meeting place for the eighties –
in a Georgian setting

Or the example of Holiday Inns in Canada:

That's the big difference between the
present and the past

You know nowadays that when you reach
your destination, there'll be a better
place to stay.

Unlike earlier generations of travellers
in Canada, you won't be a few years early.

These longer extracts demonstrate that, just as we cannot jump
straight into the introduction, we cannot jump straight into the
ending, either. Members of the audience need a little time to
gather together their thinking, away from whatever details in the
central portion have caught their individual interest.

In the most rounded of videos, that often quite brief
re-focusing period has a logical link back to the hook. It is most
obvious, perhaps, in The Brewery example, with the return of the
phrases about 'kings and dreamers', and 'leaving his mark'.

The complete video structure has thus become:

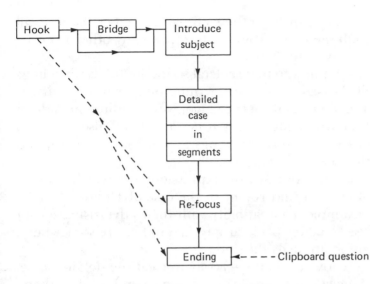

A lot of people will tinker with the words we put within this framework by the time the video has been completed. But get the frame right, and gratifyingly few will even comment on that, let alone try to change it.

A director once said to me: 'However much I might have to change your words, I can always rely on the structure you provide.'

She meant it as a compliment. Not being a writer herself, and having in that respect the sensitivity of a brick, she rather overlooked the disparaging nature of the remark about the words. But the principle behind what she said is correct. Successful videos are vertebrate animals, with strong skeletons. Create the right structure, and much of the rest will follow of its own accord.

How a writer converts that framework into a script is a matter of personal taste. We all have ways in which we prefer to work. In addition, there will be occasions when the hook is obvious even before the brief is over, or an especially potent visual suggests itself for an ending well before the central section has been considered.

I can therefore only say how helpful I find it to carry the idea of a skeleton through to the scripting itself. I will take seven or eight sheets of paper, draw a vertical line down the centre (for pictures on the left, words on the right) and number them. I will then go through the notes from the brief, and any other material the client may have supplied.

As I read, I will put into that skeletal script the subject headings for the 'detailed case in segments', writing them where I judge at that moment they will come in the video. New headings are added as I go, and the order juggled as necessary. I will also jot down detailed points under those headings as I encounter them, and any visuals that seem appropriate.

I add in, too, any phrases or expressions for which I know already I will have to find room. In the case of Holiday Inns in Canada, for example, compatibility with their advertising meant that the phrase 'A better place to stay' had to feature somewhere, and most sensibly towards the end.

The more creative elements – a way to treat the detailed case, the hook and the ending – get written down when I think of them. Sometimes they are there before any of the other bones. Sometimes they are prompted by the analysis of my notes. Sometimes they have to be reluctantly prised out of some mental recess when virtually everything else is complete. But at least the particularly daunting part, getting started, is behind us if we deal with it this way.

I have very little sympathy for the poseur author who bleats how difficult it is to be faced with a blank sheet of paper every morning. I realize someone writing fiction might feel that you should not force the process, but I cannot help wondering why they remain writers if they find the work so depressing.

For the corporate writer, however, the blank sheet of paper complaint is never valid. Even if the creative muse (take your pick, but I reckon ours is Calliope) is unwilling, there is always structure and factual detail to be getting on with.

Since we have not initiated the process, doubts about forcing it are really out of place.

A fortune awaits the scientist who discovers exactly how the creative muse achieves her results through our brains. Being at all creative is a frustrating gift, because it can be so inconsistent and unpredictable. Most writers of my acquaintance have just learned to accept that at some point they come up with ideas whose source they cannot identify.

It is, I suppose, one of the things which sorts the writers from the non-writers, and the top of the profession from the rest of us.

That does not mean, however, that we are powerless to assist the creative process. Certainly in the corporate field there are two positive steps we can take.

The first is to extend our experience whenever we can, because there will always be a way to draw on it at some later point. Eleven years in the Navy brings maritime and military hooks readily to my mind. Travel in that career and subsequently prompts geographical frames, and an abiding interest in history encourages historical analogies. Work as a management consultant allows me to make business comparisons. And so on.

This is not a list of prerequisites. Everyone brings their own personality and experience to bear. Living in rural communities. Working with charitable bodies. Going to meetings of societies. Attending reunions. Experiencing the architecture of an ancient university town as an undergraduate, or the mountains and canyons of New York as a child. A passion for railways, or for roses, for Mexican food or German wine, for topiary or mountaineering. All these, and all of the rest, will provide us with the first inklings of hooks and treatments. If we give them full rein.

And if we have them at all. The unsocial reclusive writer who works best locked in a garage may not be ideally suited to corporate video.

The second positive step is to add to our awareness and knowledge by reading widely. That means not just literature, but news and comment and factual books. Do not ignore the business pages of the newspapers; or the science articles or the arts reviews, depending on inclination.

This is to our advantage in two ways. It increases the store of potential ideas for shaping the elements of a video. But more importantly, at least to an independent writer, it also allows us to extend the range of the videos on which we can work.

'Creative' people often worry clients. With good reason. There are many stories of clients being offered wildly extravagant solutions almost before the problem had been described.

We cannot expect to know more than the client on his own subject. (And keep the chortle inside you on that odd, delightful occasion when you find you do know more.) But we are more credible and more reassuring to the client if we are clearly understanding the thrust of what he is saying about his new computer, or his organization's shortcomings, or the need to combat a social problem.

We are also much more able to ask the right supplementary questions when the client does not give us a decent brief.

We cannot be chameleons. There are bound to be some video subjects which are beyond our capability (and the professional writer recognizes that early, and says so). But the reason our horizons are limited should not be because we are ostriches.

6

Words to be Spoken
Aspects of the audio half of the script

A film might just survive a cumbersome plot, a manual on screenwriting suggests, but it has no hope if the lines are clumsy, too. Giving a video a tight structure deals with the first of those possible problems. We now need to address the second.

Before we do, however, we have to decide which method(s) we are going to use for the spoken words. Sometimes the decision may be out of our hands – already taken by the producer, or dictated by the video's intended use. But most of the time we can expect to have some input, or even a wide-open choice.

The basic split is between voiceover and dialogue. Voiceover narrative has major advantages, even if it does not by any means have the corporate field to itself. It is logistically simple. It only requires an actor or actress in a recording studio for maybe an hour, long after filming is complete. Using lip-synchronized dialogue, by contrast, means more rehearsal, more direction, slower filming, more editing. It all adds up to more cost.

When several different language versions are required, voiceover is also a clear favourite. Dubbed dialogue or sub-titles do not make for effective corporate video.

Voiceover can also, as was discussed in Chapter 2, include phraseology that would for some reason be unacceptable in naturalistic dialogue. People do not talk to each other in the language of documentaries. Since so much of corporate video is factually based, it is thus no surprise that a confident, informed single voiceover is often not just the most economical answer, it is the most effective one. The audience is as comfortable with it as with the commentaries that they hear on television programmes.

It is also a flexible concept. You can have two voices for different sections of a script (although this is practised less than it used to be). Much more useful is the effect of a second voice at specific points – purporting to be a historical figure, perhaps (as in the Canadian Holiday Inns example), or quoting from a book or a poem.

You can even have two voiceovers discussing something, although that is then very nearly dialogue and can be rather an irritating technique, since it is usually such obvious artifice. It works best in humorous cases, where artifice is taken much more for granted.

Dialogue itself is unchallengable when it comes to bringing situations alive, highlighting different ways of dealing with them and demonstrating the causes and effects of actions. That is why so many training videos make use of it.

To set against that, however, is the drawback that it demands two extra layers of expertise. It must be good dialogue (and what that means is dealt with in a moment). And it has to be well acted – which may not appear to be in our province, but is to the extent that we have written anything that is difficult to say.

Training videos will in fact commonly not split at all, but employ both voiceover and dialogue. Unlike feature films, videos do not usually have the time or the subject matter for everything to be achieved through pictures and dialogue alone. We need to know swiftly who the people we are watching are, and why they are where they are, if we are not to begin to lose interest.

Use of the voiceover in this way is not an admission of defeat but a device justified by circumstances. Those of Shakespeare's plays that use a chorus do not suffer as a result. Our videos need not suffer, either.

An example of a combination is this opening to a training film geared to improving standards in a hotel group's restaurants:

An unidentified bar. The barman is working, as no-one needs a drink. There are a pair of men, a pair of women and a group of three men in the bar	*V/O* You don't even have to be part of a conversation a lot of

Focus on pair of men. Man 1 is a brash man of the world; Man 2 is smaller and easily impressed

the time to hear what's being said.

Man 1 Did you know (lowers voice after look around) that you can get some pretty fruity videos at that shop on the corner?

Man 2 No, I didn't.

Man 1 Ah, well, you see, you have to know your way around. (Lowers voice more, talks close to Man 2's ear) All you have to do is go in, talk to the dark-haired feller and say 'Do you hire out sports goods?'

Man 2 Is that all?

Man 1 Certainly. And believe me, he's got some sports there you've never even thought of....

Camera – and eavesdropping barman – moves on, to the two women

Woman Of course, when he invited me to play he had no idea I even knew what a golf course looked like. By the 9th hole I was three up, and what happens? Surprise, surprise, he's sprained his ankle, he says. The rat. I should've wrapped a golf club round his neck.

Camera moves on to group of businessmen (BM1 + 2 + 3). A fourth man is sitting apart from them, at a table with his back to them

V/O But sometimes you hear things that perhaps you'd rather not – because they could be talking about you.

BM1 The last thing you want to

do is eat in a hotel restaurant.

BM2 Absolutely right, They employ undertakers instead of waiters.

BM3 Except that undertakers are usually more presentable.

BM2 And they never know anything about the menu.

BM1 And you can die of thirst before the food comes.

BM3 And when it does, there's always a muddle sorting out who's eating what.

BM2 And I've even been in the position where my guest has been given the bill!

BM1 And I'll tell you another thing.....

The three continue talking, now unheard

V/O That's quite a catalogue of disaster. And yet it needn't be. In every case, a little effort turns potential disappointment into actual satisfaction.

Merge with restaurant at lunchtime.......

For example....

Another variation is to have a presenter talking to camera – effectively to put the voiceover on screen. This is common in training contexts, and occasionally present in educational and induction cases.

Feelings among practitioners are mixed. There are those who hold that it defeats the object of a video to have someone talking straight at you, a view towards which I incline. The emphasis easily shifts away from what the pictures are showing, and on to the presenter.

But there are others who believe equally strongly that it personalizes the video, especially in the interactive format, where the audience is one person.

The device itself has variations, particularly in training cases. One is to have the narrator move into the company being used as a case history and become, say, the financial director (while still retaining his role as guide). Another is to have an 'invisible presenter – that is, invisible to everyone around him, but visible to the audience. This is helpful in procedural training, or in busy environments such as a bank or a factory.

Another variation encountered in interactive training is to have all the characters talk to camera when needed. To an extent this is preferable to a single person doing it, because the video has abandoned the tricky twin tasks of portraying a realistic situation but having an unreal person within it, and settled for unreality.

It can all get a little too complex for its own good, though. One training film had the voiceover turn into a presenter, then join one of the characters for a discussion. A second character then arrived to make a chatting trio, and then all three of them went down the corridor to listen in on a crisis between two more characters. As in so many aspects of life, moderation helps.

People talking to camera, or not quite to camera, is also the news interview/documentary format with which we are very familiar from our television screens. The reservation voiced in earlier chapters about avoiding talking heads still applies; but given enough pictures, we can lose the talking head quickly and just continue with the voice acting in effect as a voiceover.

In normal circumstances, when the people are experts in their field, they use spontaneous speech in response to questions, and so no scripting is involved. It is usually essential, however, to have a linking voiceover, which is the best place to put the substance of the questions. (Rather than hear each question as well as answer, which is a much slower process.)

Documentary is also an exception to the normal order of writing, since – while the skeleton may exist before any interviews take place – much of the voiceover will have to be written to reflect the actual content of the interviews.

A variant on the documentary that requires a lot of skill by all concerned to pull off is simulated documentary or news reporting. It might be suitable for training emergency services, say, or teaching the skills of being interviewed on television. But now every word has to be scripted and acted, and must be as plausible as the real thing seen regularly by the audience. In particular, the emotional responses of people after accidents, crimes or natural disasters are not easy to capture accurately.

Another variant is to use snippets filmed in documentary format. Marketing or induction videos might well include scenes of employees at their place of work or under instruction, and again any speech that is recorded will be spontaneous.

The advantages are the reality of genuine people rather than actors or models, and the additional voices (and ambient sound) as a counterpoint to the voiceover. The drawback is that many people freeze when faced with a video camera, and end up sounding as mechanical as Daleks. If you find you are working with a director capable of coaxing people back into naturalness, by all means plan in such sequences.

There are three other, more marginal ways in which spoken words can be used. All of them should be approached with a little circumspection.

One is to have a character talking to himself. In the theatre, where the conventions are very different, soliloquies and asides can work well. In a realistic medium like video or television, however, they are usually either faintly ridiculous or downright distracting. Real people – at least those who are possessed of all their marbles – just do not think out loud.

It is difficult enough to write for a character laying bare his or her soul to another person. Saying the same things to oneself is hardly ever a success on screen. A rare exception, as in other instances, is comic treatment of a situation.

More practical is the idea of hearing what someone is thinking without their actually saying it: the internalized voice, as it is grandly known, the aural equivalent of the 'thinks' balloon in a cartoon. It is still artifice, in that we do not actually think in coherent word sets, but is less jarring than soliloquy.

Its most obvious employment (and over-employment) is in radio, where it is often substituting for what cannot be seen. But it has its uses in video, particularly when examining human interaction. The difference, for example, between what is said and done on the one hand, and thought on the other, can be revealing. So can hearing the thought processes that precede an action, or reflect on it afterwards.

The third of these more limited forms is what is known as 'vox pop'. This is unidentified voices collected together speaking about a subject as if answering a question that has been edited out. It is a device used in television advertising, although there the people are usually seen as well, which makes more sense. A typical use would be the voiceover saying 'Customer reaction has already been very positive' and different voices saying 'I think it's great', 'I don't know how I ever got on without it', 'I bought two straight away' and so on.

As that example shows, it is selective and often highly contrived, and a little (if any) goes a long way.

('Vox pop' should not be confused with a 'wild track', which re-creates the sound of a particular environment. It is people, unscripted, conversing as they naturally would, at a dinner party or in a queue at a bus stop. Usually this is happening on camera, anyway, being recorded as it takes place, and so is not necessary to lay down separately. But even when required – to support a tape/slide format, for example – it will scarcely ever be scripted.)

This is a broad palette of choice, and the combination that is finally chosen from all these possibilities will be determined by the objectives of the video, its intended use and the creative treatment. When it comes to writing the actual words, though, we will still be faced with only two different animals – dialogue and voiceover.

Analysing dialogue is a little bit like describing an elephant to someone who has never seen one. The more you try, the weirder it seems to become.

It is full of paradoxes. (Dialogue, not the elephant.) It is not speech – and yet it is to be spoken. It is not real – and yet it must be realistic. It is not necessarily grammatical – and yet it must be readily understandable first time.

Because we are writing the words down, it is very easy to be misled into thinking that we are producing written dialogue. But ours are words that have to be spoken. Try reading a novel's dialogue out loud, and in most cases it will sound strange – stilted, over-formal, too polished, sometimes even long-winded. That is because one of its functions is to be as readable as the rest of the prose, and not interrupt the flow for the reader.

The film director Howard Hawks underlined the difference

with his blunt comment on judging a screenplay: 'If it reads good, it won't play good.'

I believe in this context that considering dialogue not just as what it is, but as what it does, is the most constructive advice I can offer.

In every medium that uses it, dialogue has clear-cut functions to perform. But not all of them apply in all cases. Radio dialogue, for example, must identify who is present at any one time and keep that picture clear in the listeners' minds. A visual medium can show that. Indeed, the repetition of names quickly becomes an irritant.

The functions that have to be performed by dialogue we write are:

Carry the maximum factual content
Establish the character of the speaker
Be naturalistic

If it does not do any of those, it is superfluous. With our need to be economical, we should cut it without compunction.

In some circumstances, particularly dramatized videos, dialogue will also need to do one or more of these:

Move the storyline forward
Explain what has happened but not been shown
Set up the next event

The three main functions carry within them the seeds of conflict. The demands of limited time exert great pressure, and the factual content ends up in control. At the very least, the sequence becomes implausible. 'Do real people actually talk like that?' is always one of the best tests.

A supermarket training video was completely destroyed for me because in my experience people just do not walk around discussing their shopping the way the couple I was watching did. And the manner in which characters in some management training films analyse their problems in conversation demonstrates such intellectual depth that they surely should not have got into a mess in the first place.

In the worst case, the actors end up like robots because the factual content has squeezed out all characterization. This is particularly a problem in interactive video, where the video disc restrictions on time mean that individual sequences can become very short. The actors do little more than serve as voicepieces for learning points.

One interactive producer saw that as 'the real test of a good writer – getting the balance between training facts and characterization right'. Balance, again.

A programme designer called it 'the integration of the hard edge of the training and the need to keep the trainee entertained'.

We must therefore be looking for ways of establishing character easily and quickly. A refinement of the test for dialogue is 'Would this character say this at all, and if so, how would he or she say it?' If we do not know very much about the character, we cannot answer either question properly. As a consequence, the dialogue will lose much of its impetus.

Even though we are considering dialogue, we should not lose sight of the fact that we are working in a visual medium. A radio writer has to establish character through the words. In video, let the pictures do all they can.

When it is relevant, write in the way people are dressed, their age, their mannerisms, their expressions, the movements they make through a scene. They are part of your creation, not just the director's.

But avoid the cleverness of the novelist. Descriptions provoking a wry smile – such as H.E.Bates's remark that he could not tell whether two people were men or women except that one of them had a beard – are out of place in a script.

Then concentrate on using the words to reveal aspects of character that cannot be seen, and consolidate those that can.

Consider a couple of characters from a BMW customer-care video. One was an elderly motor enthusiast, nostalgic for the past. The factual point in the sequence (from which the dialogue that follows is an extract) is that the Service Adviser should attempt to narrow down the nature of a fault on a customer's car.

| SERVICE ADVISER | What exactly is the problem, Mr Wakeman? |
| WAKEMAN | I think it's running too rich. That's what it looks like, anyway. |

SERVICE ADVISER	In the 535i the fuel/air mixture is controlled by a computer.
WAKEMAN	Most things seem to be. Time was when a driver could make all those adjustments himself....
SERVICE ADVISER	It could be an electronic fault. Do you a lot of town driving?

It is brief, but there is enough for an actor to get to grips with, without the factual message being lost. (It was just a bonus that the part of Wakeman was played by the delightful Desmond Llewelyn, the 'Q' of the James Bond films. That was only decided long after the script was signed off.)

The second character was a dynamic, power-dressing female executive. In an early sequence she storms up to the desk, and the Service Adviser unwisely decides that attack is the best form of defence. The point is how the first words you say influence the way the customer reacts.

SERVICE ADVISER	Right, madam, what's your problem?
FEMALE EXEC	My problem up till now was lorry drivers who don't look where they're going. But it's being run a close second by people who ask idiotic questions.
SERVICE ADVISER	All I was going to say was, it seemed -
FEMALE EXEC	Are you going to take my car in for a service or shall I go somewhere where I might be treated properly?

At any time subsequently, we would know that the lady does not suffer fools at all, let alone gladly. But again the training point – don't pre-judge a situation – was still there.

These layers of character introduced through the dialogue not only make the video more watchable, they are a great help to the actors.

The last of the main requirements, to be naturalistic, is the easiest to state and the hardest to define. But if the audience stops to think, they will remember that they are not looking at something real. These are pretend people in a pretend situation.

The more we can make those people talk as they might in real life, the more likely it is we will sustain the illusion for the viewer.

So while dialogue is stripped of all the padding of conversation, it still has its jaggedness. People are interrupted – as happens to the service adviser above. People do not listen silently, they react vocally as well as facially when someone else is talking. (Compare most amateur stage productions with most professional ones. In the latter, everyone acts all the time. Amateurs tend to stop acting while they wait for their next line, which is not what real people do.)

While dialogue is never random because it is fulfilling a function, it is in the language of everyday speech, not that of the function. It is the difference, taking another BMW example, between 'Constructing a garage on a road as busy as this was not very intelligent, was it?' and the line actually used, 'Wonderful site for a garage, this is, on a road that lorries use for a racetrack'.

Some individual characters will speak with sophistication and a wider vocabulary. Sherlock Holmes says 'You will realize that among your many talents dissimulation finds no place' to Dr Watson, not 'You know you're a lousy actor', because it is *in character*. Everyone's speech patterns are defined by their character, personality, upbringing and mood. 'Every character,' as an actor remarked, 'is idiosyncratic in some way.'

A vicar does not have to be a caricature to be identified by friendly, unaggressive speech. A soldier does not have to swear all the time, but what he says will be littered with the jargon of his trade. The shy, the brash, the worried, the jubilant all talk differently.

New circumstances will cause changes, too. Banter across an office with colleagues will not produce the same language as a meeting with clients or a private dinner with friends.

All this relies on what is meant by having an ear for dialogue. People do not talk the way we do, and do not all talk alike. Part of the experience we should be distilling into our writing is what we have heard of other people's ways of expressing themselves.

In our search for economy, a helpful common factor among many people is that they converse in a clipped way, low on words but high on content:

A   Sorry I was out when you called in yesterday.

B   No problem. My fault for not phoning first.
A   Want a coffee before the meeting?
B   Please.
A   Fraid we've only got a machine here.
B   I'll survive.
A   Good journey?
B   Piece of cake. Don't know where all the traffic had gone.
A   Just don't try that road on a Monday. We'll be using that office.
B   Right.

It's not great art; but it is naturalistic dialogue.

Someone who has to speak it as his profession put it this way: 'When you first read some dialogue, if it's not very good you find a voice inside says "I don't believe this, nobody would ever say that, it's not human, it's only nearly human". Good dialogue has the DNA of the character in it that gives it the breath of life.'

A tall order? Perhaps. But, like the elephant, you know it when you see it.

The demands of characterization disappear when writing a voiceover. Indeed, one of the advantages of a narrative soundtrack is its neutrality. The audience is not distracted by personalities, and gets on with listening. It should not 'be jolted by the voice drawing attention to itself', as one specialist expressed it.

There are other demands placed on us, however. A good voiceover has a story to tell, and must do so in a readily assimilable way. It must contain all the factual content that the client wants but not crowd out the pictures with too many words. It must be fluent but highly structured, pointed but not too pushy.

The major benefit to us as writers is that we are no longer required to be naturalistic. We have greater scope to use words and phrases that have more in common with writing than with speech. There is often a virtue in a deliberately arresting or pregnant expression which would appear uncomfortably artificial in dialogue.

So you can talk of the relationship between the United States and the Philippines as being 'forged in a colonial war, tempered in a world war'. A design for a bridge can be ascribed to 'man's restless ingenuity'. A timeshare estate can become 'a sanctuary of high standards'. In Dubai 'traditions are cherished'. A conference organizer is the one 'setting the standards for others to follow'. The Savoy is 'a giant among hotels – but with the gentle touch'.

A time management training film can advise being 'ruthless with time but gracious with people'. A video about the environment can show how 'the hand of man enhances the work of nature'.

In grammatical terms, we have three useful groups of weapons. The first are the verbs that provide the pivot points for the text. Development which 'disfigures' the countryside. The need to 'aspire' to greater things. Services that are 'tailored' to each client. Action that will 'regenerate the city centre'. The freedom to 'chart our own course'.

The second are the adjectives which, chosen and placed with care, will carry much more weight than might be expected of a single word. Strategic. Soul-less. Sophisticated. Surprising. Distinctive. Desolate. Deceptive. Harsh. Welcoming. Vigorous. Unprecedented. Meandering. And hundreds more.

And the third are the adverbs which refine what we are saying. Justly proud. Superficially attractive. Deservedly famous. Painstakingly planned. Delicately balanced.

But the requirement that the words have to be spoken is still the overriding one. The voiceover must therefore be pruned of fat, and packaged in units that are short and uncomplicated while still being self-contained.

For business-oriented videos, there must be no relapsing into the stale, flat prose known as business-ese. It is a struggle to read, and even worse to listen to. Particularly worth avoiding is the vocabulary that uses the longest possible words (ascertain, necessitate, envisage, exacerbate). Similarly undesirable is the combination of the passive and the anonymous 'it'. ('It is intended to complete the project' therefore becomes 'We intend to complete' or 'The project should be completed'.)

One other aspect had not occurred to me before it was drawn to my attention by a voiceover artist. 'Have you noticed – wildlife, materials, children, education, travel – the words from all those worlds are pleasurable to speak? But in the computer and medical and technical worlds, they are hard-edged, and more difficult to get your tongue around.'

I had not noticed. He has made me more alive to the problem of scripting too many technological or technocratic words close together.

One helpful difference between corporate scripts and TV documentary is the optional use of the first person plural. However much the hook and bridge may be better for being written in general terms, the detailed case might lend itself to making the transition to 'we'. Obvious in internal communication and induction, it often strengthens the ending in other cases as well if we personalize the script that way.

One marketing script concluded: 'Others may make their professionalism more obvious. We just get on with *being* professional.'

In the same way the training context can use 'you'. Obvious, again, when there is a presenter talking straight to camera, 'you' can also be used successfully by a voiceover.

It can, however, become too sanctimonious. Someone who is always telling you how to do it can get rather tiresome. A proposal writing video recognized this, and decided to take the problem by the horns. The narrative device used, yet another variation, was a wise and always unseen narrator directly advising the characters on screen, who then held conversations with him. At the end, two characters discussed what a know-all this voice was – even though they had successfully taken his advice.

The more normal way out of this situation is to alternate where it is possible with the more companionable 'we'. As happens, indeed, in this book. After all, when writing a video *you* are not faced with problems that *I* have already solved. *We* all have to solve them afresh in each script.

Knowing whether what we have written works as the spoken word is not easy. But no better alternative exists than reading it aloud.

If we have difficulty when we do that, it does not follow that the voiceover artist or the actors will. It should, however, encourage us to review the text. In particular we should be looking for three things. Are there any phrases or sentences that are too big to say comfortably in one breath? Do any sections sound long-winded, over-formal or otherwise unnaturalistic? And can we identify where we want emphasis which is not yet contained within the words?

Even though the temptation is to read it as a continuous piece, think of it as it will be, with its accompanying pictures. Do those pictures have enough space? Is there air between the words? Above all, and most commonly, can we cut back on the words anywhere?

It is idle to ignore the fact that writing the spoken word is, to an extent, a talent. That applies especially to dialogue and characterization. If it did not, we would all be Neil Simon or Alan Plater or Hart and Kaufman. But that does not mean that corporate video is therefore closed to all but a few.

What has to be recognized is the effort needed to make the words work. The shaping and reshaping to achieve the best result is a craft skill that has much in common with the potter's wheel. For corporate video, the advent of the word processor has been a great boon.

This is, however, a lesson widely unlearned. Verbose and stodgy scripts are still common, and the videos made from them never more than passable.

If a video fails to achieve great heights, at least let it not be because we have weighted it down with excess baggage.

7

Completing the Script
Bringing all the elements together

Famous sayings have an odd capacity for being inaccurate. Just as there never was a line 'Play it again, Sam', nor an 'Elementary, my dear Watson', so the phrase 'Variety is the spice of life' is also misquoted.

What William Cowper actually wrote was 'Variety's the very spice of life'. But there is also a neglected second line – 'that gives it all its flavour' – which makes the quotation even more pertinent in this context. For 'life' simply read 'video'.

Visual variety in particular is what justifies the use of the medium at all. Since the demands of the factual content and the static nature of some of the unavoidable pictures are pulling in the wrong direction, we should consider every option available to us.

The most diverse and often the most useful are **real locations**. In a video about a tourist destination, that may be obvious; it is perhaps less so in one trying to raise money for a charity, or communicating the corporation's results to its employees.

Real locations fall into four main categories. There are those that are part of the reason why the video is being made – to show the place. (That is the pure tourism case, but also hotels and conference centres, among others.) There are locations that are part of the organization, such as Head Office, or other places where it does its work, such as clients' premises. There are places which relate to the narrative line. (The script cited earlier that opened in Amsterdam is one of those.) And there are those which are selected to be a backdrop for some other element of a script, such as an acted sequence.

The last of these are usually the least problematical, and are very often chosen by the writer, anyway. They are functional and mainly unspecific locations, and can be scripted as such. 'Suburban street.' 'Roadworks.' 'Busy office.'

There is really no benefit specifying such a place by name. 'The hydrofoil jetty at Como' or 'A restaurant in San Francisco's Chinatown' may be fine on a feature film's budget, but in corporate video you can forget them.

The other three categories, however – different though they can be from each other – have one thing in common. The writer should have seen them before writing the script.

This is not to provide the writer with a fun outing: the trip is more often to Milton Keynes than to Manila. (I have no wish to insult the citizens of the former, but it is an established fact that you do not travel to see the sun set on Milton Keynes Bay.) The purpose of such a location visit is to ensure that the maximum number of visual ideas is incorporated into the script.

We are not there as a surrogate director, who will – then or later – have his or her own opinions. We are there to see how we can let pictures do all they can, and where there can be moving pictures, and capitalize on that knowledge in what we write.

Head Office may be a brick and glass box – but is there a flag flying? Is the name prominent? Is the building on a busy street? Is there a contrasting building such as a church nearby? Or a sports field, or a children's playground?

The factory may be no more than a shed – but is there a part of the manufacturing process that generates sparks, or noise, or wood shavings in bizarre shapes, or rapid movement? Is there a sharp contrast between the activity within and the rolling country outside?

Is there an unusual view to be had? (The doughnut-shaped terminals of Paris Charles de Gaulle Airport, dreadfully inefficient from the passengers' point of view, are a dream for the video maker. The 747s taxi by only a few yards away.) Does the architecture of a building have any unusual angles, in both senses?

Where is the scene animated by people? Picture postcards are fine because they are static. But on video, the snow needs a skiier, the swimming pool a swimmer, the hills a hang glider.

When filming is scheduled to take place at a particular event, such as the company's annual conference, the director will have to use some initiative, and shoot on the hoof to a great extent. The writer is out of place then, and might even get in the way, and it is exceptional to be invited to attend. But it is still useful for the writer to visit the place if possible beforehand, if only to avoid scripting suggestions that the director cannot use.

Viewing real locations is also often the time when ideas present themselves for visual hooks, or for 'wow' visuals at some point in the video.

Studio shooting is most likely in training videos, although an organization will often make genuine premises available instead. After all, even places which have no downtime during the working week (hotels, continuous process factories, police stations) can usually make some sort of arrangements to accommodate filming. Everyone else could as well, if they were so inclined.

If a studio set is budgeted, however, we need to make sure that the salient features are scripted. Is there a computer screen on the manager's desk, or only a telephone? What, if anything, is happening in the background when there is dialogue or action in the foreground? But do not write in grandiloquent details that are unnecessary.

Other types of video needing a studio are rare. A nightmare or a fantasy will need special staging, as will the visual representation of a concept. But if your ideas start to look as if they involve a lot of work, check the 'creative parameters' to make sure you are not wasting your time by being too extravagant for the budget.

Library material is already plentiful, and the supply is expanding all the time. As long as you do not call for something outlandish, a director should have no difficulty finding something suitable. If you know for certain of its existence already, so much the better.

I wrote a hook for a marketing video that included Concorde, Trooping the Colour, microchip manufacture and show-jumping, and all were duly found without much trouble.

In even greater abundance is library material in the form of still photographs. This is naturally ideal for tape/slide. But even despite the normal warning about moving pictures, stills have their uses in video as well. We have to accept that only very recently has the news-gathering video cameraman become omnipresent. Before that, a stills photographer was many times more likely to record an event, and before that there were *only* stills photographers.

Black and white or sepia pictures used discriminatingly provide a useful contrast to colour video. Variety, again. Since still photography has been around for well over a century, the subject matter often contains interesting contrasts with the present day as well.

Go back even further, and the source material is only pen drawings or paintings; but in the right context it is still just as usable.

Many museums are geared up to provide photographs of their possessions. Some – such as the Imperial War Museum – actually have masses of photographic material as part of their collections. To the extent that museums make these pictures easily available, even if for a fee, they can be regarded as on a par with libraries.

Museums will often refer in this connection to their archives. But I see a practical distinction between library and **archive material**, in that the latter cannot be purchased for anybody's use, but is made available for the video. The two most helpful sources are the records kept by an organization of its own history, which can be both moving and still pictures, and the usually moving footage of its current products, processes or activities.

A video about computer graphics, for example, drew substantially on material provided by all the leading manufacturers.

Artwork is self-explanatory. Its most common use is when design plans have been made for the interior or exterior of a building, but the video is being made before the construction or renovation is complete. In a short-term internal video, though, it could easily extend to the artwork of a planned advertising campaign.

Objects is a catch-all category for anything immobile which we can shoot especially. The list of possibilities is vast: brochures, programmes, invitations, family trees, primitive surgical instruments, Roman artefacts, World War II gas masks, old versus new product packaging, illustrations in ancient books (or the books themselves).

The problem with them is again that they are essentially static, and we need to try to introduce movement if we can. Turn the pages of a book. Run down the brochure to pick out a detail. Close in on the porcelain vase, and have it on a turntable in an interesting light. Traverse across the architect's model.

Graphics is a large and still developing field. Much of the expansion comes from the much wider availability of computer graphics as its cost comes within the reach of more productions.

Computer graphics is often understood to refer only to the dramatic and complex version seen at its most sophisticated in aircraft simulators and the introductions to TV news programmes. But although few corporate budgets stretch so far, computer graphics in its literal meaning – graphics generated by a computer – offers a lot of choice. Other cheaper forms of graphics 'generators' widen it further.

Obvious applications of their output include management and company structures; graphs, bar and pie charts; explanations of how technology works; and procedural or activity flow diagrams.

Less obvious, perhaps, is its use for maps. Real maps invariably carry more information than is needed in any one video context, and just provide clutter on the screen. The only time real maps are valid, except as a prop for actors, is when the clutter is a virtue. The camera, moving like a Hitchcock reveal of the villain right at the back of a busy scene, finally homes in on a particular place which is highlighted in some way. Otherwise a simplified graphics version – that just gives the location of all European subsidiaries, say, or of Singapore within South-East Asia – is more efficient.

It is worth adding that maps are predictable and over-used. If the idea can be expressed in a short phrase ('in all five continents', 'throughout the European Community'), a static map contributes little. A sequence of historical maps of Plymouth will show how the city has grown; but putting Plymouth on an area map of southern England has less point than 'only 3½ hours by car from London'.

The map of how to get to a hotel belongs to a brochure, not a video.

It follows that, as well as being specially created, the map ought to have some reason for being used in a video. That usually means doing what a static map cannot. Highlighting motorway networks or ferry routes. Tracing an army's line of march. Adding colour or lines to show markets or demographic information. Or using the map as a frame into which other pictures are inserted.

Facts can be made visual with graphics. A particularly useful task for them is the superimposing of one image on another.

The extraordinary size of a Russian submarine, for example, was brought home to the audience by showing its length just squeezing into Wembley Stadium. The size of Rubislaw Quarry outside Aberdeen, by contrast, was demonstrated by its ability to swallow St Paul's Cathedral.

The initials **P.O.V.** offer one other visual device. Standing for 'point of view', they are used to specify that the scene is being viewed as if from the eyes of a particular person ('driver of car's P.O.V.').

It is entirely valid to include it. But its use is normally limited to dramatized sequences, and a writer should ensure that it is genuinely needed, rather than being just a twirl and a flourish.

Directors will ignore encroachments on their patch, and a fussily detailed script may be as much an irritant to them as a help. The writer's primary job is to build a solid framework. For that, visual variety is the key.

In some cases, a writer can wrestle for ages with the hook for a video, and find that in a short time the remaining details then slot neatly into place. In other instances, a structure is easy to define, but the content of the main section remains obstinately lifeless. No two scripts are ever quite the same.

One of the principal jobs at this completion stage, however, never changes. Even if we have created a video in a cold-blooded segmented fashion, we must remove all traces of that fact.

Link points are unavoidable. What we have to do is ensure that they do not jar or interrupt the flow.

The worst way is to write words that say flatly 'This is a link'. An example of that is the line 'Now let's go back to how the City developed after the Great Fire'.

The only reasonable use of such a sentence is in training videos – 'Let's look at a different sort of customer' – especially the interactive case, where the highly segmented structure is an indivisible part of the scheme of things. In marketing or education, such lack of subtlety could easily sound patronizing.

There are several better ways of making links. One is strongly to signpost the next element. 'At its centre is one of the great cities of the world – Manila.' 'There was one more travel revolution to come'. 'Even then, one more problem remains to be solved.' (Or, in the case just cited, 'The City's development after the Great Fire came in phases. Up to the end of the seventeenth century...'.)

A second way is to use the link point as a summary of what has gone before. A training video on time management did just that in reference to dealing with (so-called) crises: 'So – don't start a second fire trying to put out the first one.'

A third method is to combine the first two by underlining what has been said so far, but pointing forwards at the same time. 'But a successful present and future are not built on the record of the past alone. That is why...' 'Quality today – but also quality tomorrow. We are constantly developing new techniques....' 'Once order processing has been successfully completed in this way, transport department takes over responsibility.'

A fourth way is to emphasize the natural sequence of events, and thus make them more dramatic. This is the 'Day 3, 1400' approach applied to a developing military situation, or the sharp breaks between planning, travel, set-up and live show of a product launch.

In all of these, and all others, music can be used in support or as an alternative. But only rarely is it necessary for us to specify a music change unless we have a specific effect in mind.

Our job is to see that the words in the script are carrying the viewer forward smoothly, without bumps at the joins. It is another good reason for testing a script by reading it aloud.

Humour has so far only been mentioned in passing. That is mainly because it is capable of misfiring in the wrong hands.

It is fiendishly difficult to judge correctly what will make people laugh. That is why good situation comedy writers are in such demand for television. Their audiences are admittedly measured in millions, and ours in hundreds or, at best, thousands, but the problem is the same.

Even when we are targeting a closely defined group – shop assistants, say, or stockbrokers – there is no way of being certain we know what their sense of humour is. The uncongenial environments in which people watch corporate video can also be less than conducive to being amused.

In addition, for the many videos that are used in more than one country, humour can travel badly. An excruciatingly unfunny introduction to a German telephone technique video was not directed at me, and so I have to give it the benefit of the doubt. There was certainly plenty of doubt.

For the same reason, some American cinema films never achieve the success abroad that they enjoy at home, because of the heavy reliance on native brands of humour.

Integrating humour into the whole video is a policy decision for the client, and there are differing views and conflicting evidence. Even leaving aside the sort of subjects that are too serious to be joked about, there are many people who say that to deal humorously with factual corporate subjects is to run the risk of demeaning or ridiculing them.

There are others who will maintain that messages are more readily remembered when they are couched in an amusing way. That is, after all, the basis for the Video Arts style of film, and certainly there is reason to believe that humour can soften the content of a training video, and make it more acceptable.

In marketing, by contrast, my own experience is that humour is very much the exception. What discourages many people who might otherwise be prepared to use it is that when it does not strike home, the negative audience effect is often worse than if humour were not there at all.

Even if we are only using humour in small quantities, therefore, it is close to fail-safe in the corporate context if it passes three tests. Is it relevant? Are we keeping it brief? And does it stand on its own without audience reaction?

Relevance means that the content remains valid even if the viewer does not find it amusing. It is in deference to the factual nature of corporate video. The more extreme the humour (such as slapstick), the more likely it is to fail this test.

Brevity is to prevent mental withdrawal by viewers who at home would switch channels away from comedy not to their taste, but who in a corporate context must stick with it to the – as they would see it – bitter end. If we do not dwell on the point, we run much less risk of losing the viewers' sympathy, and with it their attention.

One case that worked because it was brief was a customer-care video which suggested that taking a certain action would only result in egg on our face. The actor on screen at that moment then got precisely that, an egg broken on his forehead. The phrase was so familiar that complete surprise was achieved by taking it literally for once. But the camera did not linger. It moved on long before the thoroughly messy reality of a broken egg running down a face took the edge off the joke.

Another successful instance was a running joke in an airport video of a double bass (actually a piece of baggage) that kept appearing in very brief shots in all sorts of unlikely places.

The third test, audience reaction, is less straighforward. Painful though the hyena laughter of sitcom studio audiences can be to a television viewer at home, it is (mostly) a genuine response to the live performance. Strip away the audience, and willy-nilly the effect will change. If the humour relies on timing, it will seem more strained. If it relies on the vocal contribution of the audience, it will seem exaggerated in silence, and perhaps embarrassing.

Even if we ape a sitcom's structure in a video, we cannot draw support from a live audience's responses. We need the sort of humour embedded in character or situation that the cinema employs, with the storyline running on independent of reaction.

For a voiceover, our aim in any case is more likely to be to raise a smile than a laugh. The single well-placed phrase, as always, is much more use to us than a series of relentless gags. A maker of tennis courts turned to making runways when, 'in 1939, people had rather more on their minds than tennis'. At Sea World in Florida, the voiceover said, after a pause: 'Sharks are *not* an endangered species.' Economy of words, again.

If I seem to be reluctant to give humour much credit, it is only because experience makes me cautious. I have sat through more disasters in this respect than successes. When humour works, it is memorable. When it does not, it is also memorable, but for entirely the wrong reasons.

I have simply come to believe that some video makers could be a little more honest about how much the audience is likely to be amused by their off-beat sense of humour.

Humour is optional. But some of the words in the script may not be.

If we accept that in corporate video the clients have the final say – as we logically must – there will be times when our judgement will be overridden by theirs.

Some of that will be fully justified, because of our lack of detailed knowledge of the specialist expressions used in that particular trade. We write 'working clothes', and it gets changed to 'workwear'. We say 'operator', and they prefer 'operative'. We script 'lorry', and it ends up as 'truck'.

But sometimes the case will be less clear-cut. The client will insist on including facts or statements that we think are unnecessary or inappropriate.

That is life. Only when the new words weaken the overall structure or fundamentally alter a particular effect or characterization do I believe it is worth throwing up barricades against such change. Differences of opinion on the use of words are commonplace even in purely creative writing. In our sort of factual, targeted work, both the content and the text have to be up for discussion.

Given that situation, our task as professionals is to absorb those changes into the script as seamlessly as possible.

Probably the biggest hazard is so-called shopping lists, where we are left naming one feature or product or service after another. One alternative the client may accept is the 'from...to' device, which demonstrates variety by taking two contrasting examples. Another is to introduce the list with a single statement – 'with a comprehensive range of support services', 'a wide choice of leisure activities' – and let the pictures show the truth of the statement. A third is to divide the list into two, the predictable and the unexpected, and use the 'not only...but also' technique.

Clients unused to the spoken word are likely to see nothing wrong with using lots of numbers and statistics in the script. Apart from warning about their ability to date a script, we should be suggesting rounding those figures up or down, or finding another way to express them.

'A market share of 19.7%' becomes 'We sold one car in every five'. 'Sales of $30.9 million' can be 'Sales of over $30 million'. 'Our turnover is up 96% on last year, but costs have only increased by 47%' is slicker as 'Our profit this year has increased at twice the rate of our costs'. The fact that 'the gross national product of California is $xxx billion' has more impact as 'California has the sixth largest economy in the world'.

This is not cheating, or being sparing with the truth. It is turning numbers, which the brain dislikes accepting through the ears in large quantities, into ideas.

Single words also express ideas, and some of those (both the words and the ideas) can seem hackneyed. 'Unique', for example, is likely to be called for in any marketing script. In fact I do not have any problem with the word, if it is correct. I can sympathize with the view of one producer that such a script is potentially flawed if 'unique', or at least the concept of uniqueness, is *not* there. (On the basis that, if nothing is unique, what differentiates the subject of this marketing video from any other of its sort?)

I only cavil when I am encouraged to write 'almost unique'.

Many other absolute adjectives, like 'definitive' and 'unprece-dented', cause me equally little heartache as long as they can be truthfully applied. I get more concerned by the hyperbolic use of words like 'ultimate' ('the ultimate experience'), 'unbeatable' ('unbeatable value') and 'never' ('we shall never see their like again') because of the impossibility of knowing if the statement is accurate.

A lot of other strong descriptive words – remarkable, astonishing, surprising – have a similar air of inevitability about them. The solution is usually to justify them. If a word is used alone, the accompanying pictures must genuinely surprise or astonish – it means thinking in visual terms again. Or factual support must go into the words: 'Stretched end to end, these remarkable rice terraces would reach half-way round the world.'

'Excellence' is a recurring favourite that is also difficult to avoid. It may help to define its meaning in the particular context, since it is an elastic word. It is also preferable to move from a single word to an expression ('the pursuit of excellence', 'the hallmark of excellence'). It may even be better to revert to an adjective ('these excellent results') or move into a verb ('this division has excelled itself').

The word 'quality' poses a unique difficulty. (Well, very unusual, anyway.) Clients always want to emphasize they have it. Yet the fact of saying it prompts the question why that has been necessary – is there some doubt about it? It is the 'lady doth protest too much' syndrome.

There are several options. One is to show the consistency of quality across several different services or products. Another is to indicate that quality is as high as customers expect, throwing the ball back to the viewer. (But it could be dangerous if the customers have low expectations.) A third is to define what quality means in this context – which often points us back towards 'unique' as well as descriptive words like 'impeccable' and 'first class'.

As with so many other aspects of scripting a corporate video, there is no one answer. A phrase that sounds like a tired cliché in one context can be highly effective in another. It is a matter of taste, of audience analysis, of the video's purpose and of the complementary nature of the words and pictures.

In any case, there are five creative opportunities for every one of these unavoidable words. Anyone who demands to be totally unfettered in their choice of vocabulary should be writing poetry, not corporate videos.

When we are close to completing a script, it is as well to review one more time whether we have carelessly left any unexploded bombs lying around for the time when the cameras actually roll. As an actress put it with great feeling after direct experience: 'Don't ever script in small children or performing animals.'

8
Exploiting the Medium to the Full
Ensuring the video is both individual and effective

'The tingle factor', it has been called. 'The little bit of magic' was how one producer also described it. It is those moments, sometimes tantalizingly brief, that ensure the video will be remembered.

Even those who make them dispute hotly whether videos can achieve objectives entirely alone. But all are agreed that a video must not just be understandable at the time but must have enough impact for some element of it to be retained for much longer. Only then is it likely to prompt any action later on the viewer's part. And only then can it truly be judged effective.

The need to make each video distinctive in some way has never been greater. As the number being made increases by leaps and bounds, the creative resources of the makers are stretched ever thinner. Or so, at least, it seems.

'Corporate videos are all the same' said one (prize-winning) producer; and it is not necessary to agree absolutely with such a direct statement to understand why it was made. If a conference can be convened with the title 'No More Boring Videos', it is time to review how the situation can be improved.

The search for originality can lead up blind alleys. Throw enough technological wizardry at the video, and you can certainly impress. But − rather like the clever adverts apparently made more with an eye to the industry's awards than the selling of a product − what about the client's message? Usually it slides into oblivion.

Another unhappy trend (except for the people involved, who

command sizeable fees) is the use of television personalities as on-screen presenters. The thinking behind it is obvious enough. Instead of competing with the audience's TV expectations, we pander to them. The well-known face lends credibility to the proceedings.

It can work. The various stock characters in a well-known comedian's repertoire, for example, represent different customers more amusingly than a clutch of anonymous actors. And the familiar publican from a popular series might prove useful behind a comparable bar in the video.

But in many instances the value of the newscaster or the botanist or the pop show host is very questionable. Such an individual has clearly been brought in for window-dressing reasons, which can easily cause the viewers to ask themselves why the window needs dressing. Is it otherwise too bare? It is hardly a constructive train of thought to set up.

Just as importantly, a strong personality can draw the focus on to himself (or, less commonly, herself), and divert attention away from the subject of the video.

Perhaps most dangerously of all, many people with a high public profile have as many detractors as fans. It goes with the job, and adds to their newsworthiness, but it cannot be an advantage to the client to have part of the audience turned off by a performer or broadcaster they cannot abide. We can all compile a list of television faces we have seen too much of already. The names we might personally favour stand a good chance of being on other people's unfavourite list. It is too late to discover that when the video is made.

There are more profitable lines to pursue. One is to give the audience the unusual.

That might be nothing more complex than a simple object seen at an odd angle – across a maze of rooftop TV aerials, perhaps, or through a ship's hawsepipe or from a couple of inches above street level.

The unusual can also appear as words. One producer believes a corporate video should always tell something to the audience which they did not know before. It is the sort of line included in a video about St Paul's: 'The only English cathedral to be completed in its architect's lifetime.' (Even though it took 35 years to build.)

More usefully still, we can draw on the power of the

unexpected. The cobbled street we are in could be anywhere – until we are suddenly stopped by a rampart, and a steep drop beyond it, and learn for the first time that this is a virtually intact medieval walled town.

The rock face we are looking at appears to be like any other – until it is shattered by an explosion, and tells us this is a quarry.

The 'pull-back reveal' also provides surprise. Two old men are playing chess. Nothing remarkable in that. But as we pull back, we see they are doing so aboard a small boat on a lake, or next to the lions' cage at the zoo.

One plain cross is moving, but unsurprising. Pulling back to find it is one of thousands of identical crosses is a shock.

Anyone who has seen *Gone With The Wind* will know the extraordinary scene, filmed the same way, when Scarlett O'Hara discovers a whole army of wounded in the town square.

The reverse process is also powerful. A nondescript scene takes on new life as we go in closer, and the camera eventually finds something of significance: the name printed on a pedestrian's carrier-bag, say, or the same pair of shoes we keep encountering without knowing the identity of the owner.

We can play tricks to create the unexpected, too. The bare brick of an unfinished entrance hall in a palace can instantly transform to the same place completed in a riot of different coloured marble. (I was able to script that in to a video about Germany, because Herrenchiemsee Palace in Bavaria has one entrance hall completed and one uncompleted. But it is the same effect to show an empty exhibition hall and merge it with that same location seen in the middle of a hectic trade fair.)

Bearing in mind the nature of the medium we are using, we should also look for the visually memorable. The light streaming in through the high windows of the Great Hall of the castle, creating ghostly patterns in the smoke from the log fire in the huge fireplace. The airliner flying with all its cabin lights already on, as a deep red sun sets behind it. The orange red of the morning sun making a silhouette out of the towers of the Manhattan skyline. The action of a racehorse at full gallop, but shown in slow motion.

Close-up can be useful here – showing the skill of the craftsmen's hands, or the scary faces of carved gargoyles, or the manic activity of an automatic bottling process.

We can also create tension visually. The island of stillness in a sea of movement, for example – the solitary child in a busy playground – must have a reason to be there, and we want to know what it is.

All that these examples are doing, though, is paying particular attention to the seven key principles of video. If we do that, the unusual, the unexpected and the memorable will often taken care of themselves.

Letting the **pictures** do all they can means giving preference to the visual whenever it is possible. If a hotel overlooks Central Park, then it is the view from the bedrooms that matters, not the bedrooms themselves.

Do not describe the effect of a thermal imager: switch one on, to change the darkness to eerie grey, and reveal the tanks and soldiers previously hidden by the night.

Use the camera to tell the audience that people are farmers or fishermen or miners or nurses. Look for visual detail to establish location in an interesting way. The angles and arches of an old church. The archaic uniform of the attendants on the door. The contrast at the heart of many cities between an unpretentious working river and graceful or striking buildings.

Alfred Hitchcock used to be proud of working with the cutting of the finished film already clear in his mind – indeed, already recorded in the script. But he was a director. A writer is unlikely to win much sympathy by scripting such a high level of editing. However, if a particular visual effect requires a sharp cut, by all means say so.

The pilot's finger on the firing button followed immediately by the external view of the missile firing from its launcher should be scripted. So should the sudden juxtaposition of empty tropical beaches and packed urban streets.

Not the least important, look for a visual hook.

This underlines once again the requirement placed on the thoughtful corporate video writer to think in visual terms – and whenever possible to see locations before the script is written.

If the **ideas** are expressed in the right words, they, too, will linger in the mind. ARC sought to demonstrate how it restored its quarries after extracting the stone by talking of only 'borrowing the land'. British Airways underlined how each action by its employees is like that of an athlete, every perfomance judged on its merits, 'for the judges have no memory'. The World Computer Graphics Association lodged the idea of how vital they believe computer graphics to be by concluding a video: 'Helping us to understand the present, and to create the future.'

Shaping and honing the central idea running through a video into one crisp, easily remembered sentence is perhaps the most important single contribution that the writer can make.

Combining the two core elements of words and pictures brings to the fore again the need for them to be **complementary**. Why list the famous people buried in the crypt, when their names are emblazoned on their tombs? Why explain this is a swimming pool, or an airport, or a hospital, when that can be seen immediately? Duplication is a waste of resources, and, more importantly, a way to irritate or bore the audience.

Almost always it is the words that prove to be superfluous. The most consistent criticism from all the people I spoke to during the preparation of this book was that scripts are too wordy. Those who have to speak the heaps of verbiage feel particularly strongly about it. 'It's difficult enough to say – it must be so boring for the poor people who are watching,' said an actress.

And an actor expressed it this way: 'I'm told it's a ten-minute video. But then if the script's heavy when it comes out of the envelope, 15 pages or more, you know it's not going to be any good. There aren't going to be any pauses, and there's going to be a fight between the pictures and the words.'

The economical use of words is a virtue in its own right. But in addition, the fewer we have, the greater the chance of those being heard and registered. It is easier to make a point when words and pictures are complementary.

Take the opening of a script about nutrition:

Library pictures of the best aspects of Victorian life – great houses, lots of leisure time, garden parties, balls, picnics, elegance and opulence	The quality of life is not what it was -
Sharp cut to library pictures of urban and rural poverty – dirt, overcrowding, poor housing, scraps of food	for which we should be grateful

The fact that the words have to be **spoken** is also a good reason for cutting them back. The flowing syntax of a novel or the dense vocabulary of a report may be fine on the printed page – but they are likely to be a struggle to cope with when they come in through the ears.

Again hear the heartfelt complaint of the voiceover artist: 'They're such heavy scripts – jam-packed full of jargon, or even using words that don't exist. You can't put any meaning into that.'

That is why every writer should cultivate the habit of running through a script out loud to see how it *sounds*. It is the only way to check if it works.

That is why it is always preferable to present a script to a client verbally before he reads it – so that he will first of all listen to it the way an audience will.

That is why it is so depressing to hear of a group of clients sitting around a table all silently reading different drafts of the script, and pronouncing on their relative merits on that basis alone.

Nor do we want the audience actually **reading** words if it is at all possible to avoid them. Memorable videos have rhythm and pace which may vary, but which are consistent with the overall tone and flavour. We do not want to reduce even a gentle tempo still further by putting words on the screen, and forcing viewers to become readers.

Apart from any other drawback, words are often completely static, when we should be using pictures that are **moving**.

Even inanimate objects can be given life with movement. Seen from above, the marble floor of the Manila Hotel with the name picked out in mosaic is given more point when a waiter with a tray of drinks walks across it. The tourist view of Sacré Coeur in Montmartre is made more interesting by the camera finding an airliner in the distance beyond it, and tracking it across the sky.

A warehouse is not the most fascinating building on earth. But put the camera on a trolley that travels down the central aisle, and choreograph the movement of fork lift trucks crossing the picture out of the side aisles, and you have an image of the warehouse that every viewer is likely to retain.

In principle, therefore, script in the moving rather than the static: the vehicle rather than the building, the people rather than the view, the animals in the woods rather than the trees, the factory rather than the computers. Or achieve an effect by contrast, between the moving and the static.

The mundane, such as maps, also become tolerable when they are given movement. Think of the line being drawn across a simple map superimposed on an aircraft in flight that tracks Indiana Jones's travels (in *Raiders of the Lost Ark*). And then compare it with the flat 'We have offices all over the country' map in many videos.

Even that bane of corporate video, the talking head, can be memorable given enough movement. As the complete antithesis to Alfred Hitchcock's urgent editing, all but the first couple of lines of the 'Once more unto the breach, dear friends' speech from Laurence Olivier's *Henry V* are filmed as one unbroken sequence. It is a minute and a half long. But the camera is on the move after the first few seconds, pulling back and travelling in an elliptical path to take in more and more of a scene that eventually includes parts of the ships beside the water.

Soldiers mill around their leader, others join the crowd, still others move across the line of the camera carrying banners. The tall pikes many of them are holding shift gently like stalks of corn in a breeze.

As a result, a theoretically static scene is vibrant with tension.

(We are talking principles here. I am not suggesting giving the company chairman a drawn sword and putting him on a warhorse for his half-yearly talk to the employees – although it is an attractive thought.)

Last, and by no means least, there is the impact of **sound**. The whole medium is, after all, called audiovisual, not speechvisual. It makes no sense to neglect this additional weapon in our armoury.

Just as the eye can swiftly tap into the enormous range of images in the brain's memory bank, so the ear can prompt the recall of dozens of sounds and give them meaning. You do not have to be a tennis player to know what a measured voice saying 'Fifteen-love' signifies. It is not necessary to have lived in the forests of Eastern Europe to recognize the howl of wolves. The differences between a doorbell, a telephone bell, a bell on a bus, a bicycle bell, a handbell and a church bell are all immediately obvious.

So powerful is sound, indeed, that it can come close to suppressing reality. The Imperial War Museum in London relies heavily on audio to re-create its bomb shelter experience of the Blitz. And in the Railroad Museum in Old Sacramento, the familiar doppler effect of passing a clanging crossing bell adds strongly to the feeling inside a carriage that you are moving.

In the hook of a video, therefore, sound can make it memorable by preceding the pictures – such as with the ominous rumbling and roaring of an awakening volcano. Unavoidable but unimpressive images are enhanced – as when pictures of a government file store were overlaid with the sounds of the machinery that had once been there: it was originally a cotton mill. The straightforward is strengthened – using the engine noise of an aircraft, for example. And the surprise of the unexpected is heightened when supported by sound.

In some cases, music is the most potent of all sounds. In one instance, an airline marketing video was edited – indeed, conceived and scripted – to fit exactly the pattern of the Beethoven music that was its sole soundtrack.

But if it were necessary to sacrifice all but one key characteristic of video, the one to retain would be **taking people where they cannot otherwise go**.

A training video for Midland Bank re-created as a bizarre nightmare all the negative aspects of banks that customers react against.

A marketing video for Kent took viewers all over the county in 8 minutes. Just as that for the Café Royal took in a day in its life in 10 minutes.

And at New Market Battlefield Park, in Virginia, the audience travels for 12 minutes where it is truly impossible to go: into the past. The historic involvement of 247 young cadets in a fierce Civil War engagement is evoked brilliantly, but without lavish budgets – there is, for example, no expensive set-piece reconstruction of the fighting. The reliance is placed mainly on a taut script and intelligent visualization.

It is, in fact, all that video should be. And the result is memorable.

It is a brave or a foolish person who predicts precisely what will happen to audiovisual in the next few years. But certain trends are clear.

One is that high-definition television offers picture quality so high that those who have seen it cannot adequately describe it to those who have not. But the effect on the writer is minimal. If anything, it simply draws attention to the need to think in visual terms.

Another trend is the still greater penetration of electronics into the creative areas. Pictures shot separately (a 747 and a kangaroo, say) will be both easy and cheap to combine. Electronic 'cleaning-up' of footage will be more commonplace, too. If you find you have unwittingly filmed a man with a tattoo on his arm, you can remove it and replace it with 'skin' duplicated from elsewhere in the picture. It is already cheaper to do that than to re-shoot the sequence, and the costs will presumably fall in the future.

But again, these are part of the director's province. At the most, the writer simply needs to be aware of them.

The ultimate demise of tape/slide has also been forecast, with electronic frame stores and computer-generated 'slides' being used on high-definition video. I bow to superior knowledge, but still expect little impact on the writer.

In fact, I do not yet see any reason at all to suppose that the fundamental role of the writer will change. He or she will continue to be required to produce video scripts that balance creativity with the client's objectives.

We will still be the principal providers of the raw material on the page out of which can develop a video that is, in a producer's words, 'relevant and distinctive'.

Some people will always find that easier than others: life has never been fair. But if this book helps the majority among us who are not touched with genius to create better scripts, it has at least been relevant.

If it has been in any way distinctive as well, I am well pleased. When you have 'the incurable disease', as the Roman writer Juvenal called the urge to write, realizing you have achieved what you set out to do is a source of considerable satisfaction.

Appendices

Three sample scripts

Each of these three appendices contains a complete script which I have written. To put them in perspective, there is in each case an outline of the main points of the brief, a short analysis of the thinking that led to the script, and a review after the script of any changes that were introduced into the final version (which is the one reproduced).

The satisfaction of the client and the effectiveness of the completed video when it is used are the only valid yardsticks for success in the corporate field. These scripts are chosen because they met those yardsticks. Whether or not they are also well written is up to the reader to judge.

In addition, all three scripts share a second characteristic: they underwent very little change. This was mainly because they were well briefed and had clear objectives.

They cover three of the main uses of corporate video, as follows:

A – Marketing – for Ettington Park Hotel
B – Training – for Data General Corporation
C – Internal Communications – for OCS Group

Appendix A
A marketing script

The Brief

Ettington Park, close to Stratford-upon-Avon, is one of the most successful conversions of an opulent private home into a top-class hotel. The land, and houses that have stood on it, have been in the ownership of the Shirley family for well over 900 years. The current house dates back several centuries, although it was on the Victorian rebuilding that the conversion was based.

As with any hotel, the video's core list of contents was largely predictable. The features included rooms which were individual in both shape and design. Despite major alteration of the interior to fit it for its new role, whole elements of the original house had been carefully retained. The Library became the bar. The Conservatory was the entrance lobby. The former chapel, with its stained glass, was the dining-room. There was also a modern leisure centre, and conference rooms.

The character of the house itself was to be emphasized, naturally enough, and also its location. The latter was to include mention of important attractions within easy reach: Stratford, Warwick Castle and Blenheim Palace.

There were two audiences. The primary one was the independent traveller in the United States, looking for somewhere different to spend a holiday and going to a travel agent for advice. Copies of the video were to be sent to selected travel agents in the United States for them to show to prospective customers.

The secondary audience was senior management in the UK, looking for a quiet and up-market location for small conferences (not more than 40 people).

The answer to the clipboard question, aimed at the primary audience, was 'I'd like to go there – it's really English and it's got style'. (On the basis that to many Americans, who live in a country which understands the concept of service, being English and having style could easily be thought mutually exclusive ideas.)

At the time of the brief, a draft brochure was in preparation, which provided a lot of detailed information that supported the brief and the walk round the premises. There were also two books: one a history of the house itself, the other a history of the parish of Lower Ettington which included the house. They were the source of two very apposite quotations, as well as of more background material.

Another video existed, made by 'the friend of a friend'. Its flavour can be accurately gauged by the opening, which showed a picture of the house looking very like Castle Dracula accompanied by the words 'This is Ettington Park'. That video was quite reasonably kept under lock and key, and shown to no-one.

Analysis

The central section contained two elements which had to be handled carefully, because they could otherwise cancel each other out. The age of the building could easily be perceived as meaning old-fashioned; the modern facilities could be taken as being the same as any other hotel. It was to deal with both of these that the idea of the English country house was adopted.

Location, while important, had to be considered in general terms for the primary audience. It was for that reason the phrase 'the heartland of England' was employed.

Similarly, it was sensible to assume that the primary audience would not be familiar with the detail of English history, so the hook needed to be something which any viewer would recognize. That was why the video opened with Shakepeare.

The bridge was to regard Shakespeare's words as a tangible legacy of the past, and then suggest others, such as buildings –

leading us on towards the specific building with which we were dealing. Quite deliberately, it was over a third of the way into the script before the name was mentioned. This was in order to suggest in general terms that this was a place worth visiting, before getting too specific.

The secondary audience had to be reassured at some point that the conference facilities they needed were indeed in the hotel. But it was more important that they should register location, which they could do easily, and quality, which was being presented to the primary audience as well.

The Script

Title page of *Richard II* Retain as frame, with other pictures superimposed centre-screen	*Alternate voice* This royal throne of kings
Sunrise over countryside	This scepter'd isle This earth of majesty
Sunlit countryside	This seat of Mars, this other earth, demi-paradise,
Ruined castle	This fortress built by Nature for herself against infection and the hand of war. This happy breed of men,
Half-timbered cottage	This little world, This precious stone set in the
Lake at Blenheim	silver sea, which serves it in office of a wall, or as a
Warwick Castle	moat
Elizabethan house	Defensive to a house against the envy of less happier lands
Open fields	This blessed plot,
Woodland, with shafts of sunlight through trees	This earth, this realm, this England.

Merge from page of play to play being acted	*Voiceover* The incomparable quality of Shakespeare's plays keeps them as fresh today as when they were written.
Views of rural Warwickshire	But his is not the only legacy of the past that we marvel at still.
Shakespeare memorial in Bancroft Gardens, Stratford General views of Stratford, including Royal Shakespeare Theatre and Avon	And nowhere do we have more cause to marvel than close to his birthplace, in Stratford-upon-Avon
Cotwolds Open country Villages	This is the heartland of England
	Where some of the finest buildings in the country match the richness and variety of Shakespeare's words.
Warwick Castle	Solemn castles
Blenheim Palace	Gorgeous palaces
Ettington, not yet identified, in distance	And fine country houses.
Ettington, closer to	And only a few miles from Stratford, there is one country house in particular
Grounds, emphasizing size and greenness	It is set in forty acres of parkland,
River	through which runs the River Stour
Church in grounds	
	Land owned by the same family, the Shirleys, since before the Norman Conquest.
Elements of older building in current Ettington Park	It is a building that incorporates elements of its predecessors on the same spot – for as early as the 1600s a writer could record that
Ancient book	
Early prints, drawings – 1738, 1821	*Alternate* This is a very ancient mansion-house, built so long ago

(Music change)
Ettington 1864

View up drive

Establishing shot, modern
Ettington Park
Introduce full name, logo
Different shots of exterior

Prints of life in a country
house, nineteenth century

Examples of different
bedrooms
Examples of angles, beams,
windows
Example of variation
Examples

Examples of bathroom
fittings, hairdryer, extras such
as cabinet TV
Conservatory

that the memory, by the revolution of so many ages, is utterly lost and forgotten.

Voiceover In the last century it was enhanced again, and given its present distinctive form. And it is the elegance and grandeur of that time a century ago that was, in 1984, restored.

This is Ettington Park.

A hotel in name – but in spirit, still a country house.

For while traditionally you lived very comfortably in an English country house, you also enjoyed a way of life far removed from that of an impersonal modern hotel
Here there is comfort
In every one of the large, and individual, bedrooms and suites
– for no two rooms are the same

or have the same decor
But all have the same high quality of furnishings
and every modern amenity.

What other hotel has its main entrance within a delightful conservatory dating back a century and a half?

and the same comfort and style that are found in each of the public rooms as well?

Great Drawing Room	The Great Drawing Room, with its fine Rococo ceiling
Bar	The Library Bar
Little Drawing Room	The Little Drawing Room
Restaurant	The Restaurant, with its wood panelling
Chapel	And the Dining-Room, in the former chapel – perfect settings to enjoy the finest cuisine.
Examples of dishes	
Staff in action	All this is complemented by the quality of service that befits a country house – courteous unobtrusive impeccable –
Pick up details of house – windows, stained glass, carving, statuary	reflecting exactly the attention to detail that has been lavished over the years on the house itself.
Recap early country house pictures	But it is not enough just to recapture the comfort and style of a more leisurely age.
	Ettington Park has drawn on the best the twentieth century can offer to provide a leisure centre
Representative pictures throughout leisure centre	with a swimming pool spa bath sauna and billiards room to supplement outdoor activities
Example	such as fishing
Example	tennis
Example	riding
New shots of hotel grounds	or just relaxing in the peace and quiet of the gentle Warwickshire country.
Reprise establishing shot	Ettington Park's distinction is present in the each of the

	facilities available to those who need to mix business with pleasure.
South Room, emphasizing features	The splendid South Room
Long Gallery, emphasizing unique construction	and the spectacular Long Gallery
	provide remarkable and memorable venues for every kind of meeting – meetings which will be supported
Meetings staff in action	by the same high standard of service evident throughout Ettington Park.
Recap bedroom, leisure centre	Of course, every new hotel boasts its luxury
Library bar, other public rooms	But hardly any can demonstrate such character as well.
	A traveller in the early 1800s speaks for us still:
Overall view exterior	*Alternate* I love old houses best, for the sake of
Example at Ettington	good thick walls that do not let the wind blow in, and
Bedroom example	out-of-the-way polyangular rooms with
Long Gallery	great beams running across the ceiling,
Example	chimney pieces,
South Room	and huge fireplaces
Cotswold landscape	*Voiceover* Many of the past's greatest achievements are sadly lost to us now.
	All the more reason, then, to cherish those we still have in the heart of England.
Stratford	
Posters and extracts of some famous plays	The plays of Stratford's most celebrated citizen
Warwick Castle	The great medieval fortress at Warwick

Blenheim Palace	The magnificent home of the Churchills, Blenheim Palace
Overall exterior shot of Ettington	And the classic English country house
Superimpose logo	Ettington Park.

Comment

As with any marketing script, considerable discussion went on over the choice and placing of individual words. 'Finest cuisine', for example, reflects second thoughts — it had originally been 'finest French — as well as traditional English — cuisine'. The outdoor activities were shown, but it was also felt necessary to name them. And so on.

But those were details, and in fact there were not many instances of them.

The structure was essentially unchanged. However, the original hook had used brief excerpts from several Shakespeare plays, including *Richard II*, with visuals illustrating each one that were very similar to those in the final version. The different plays were replaced by the one, longer, speech, because of the specific reference to England contained within it, and the fact that the visuals lent themselves just as well to illustrating what a single voice was saying.

In addition, a reference to the Romans was deleted. Their principal visible legacy in the area was a road, which sat uncomfortably with all the talk of splendid buildings.

Considerable latitude was left to the director on the visual side for two reasons. He was bound to take his own direction, anyway, since the building was so full of fascinating details, both inside and out. And in one or two instances I could not be more specific, because at the time I took the brief, parts of the hotel were barely recognizable in the building work that was under way.

Appendix B
A training script

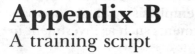

The Brief

Data General Corporation (DG) is a major minicomputer manufacturer with headquarters in the United States. Its substantial European operations, carried on in fifteen countries, are centred in Paris.

As part of a programme of improving and sustaining the quality of their service to customers, the theme of 'Commitment to Excellence' had been selected. The video was intended to have the same title. It would sometimes be used alone, sometimes within the body of a training course, and was aimed particularly at those employees who rarely, if ever, had face-to-face contact with customers. The main ones mentioned were receptionists, telephone operators, administrative staff, engineers, storemen and managers.

Examples of the sort of areas it would be useful to focus on were speed of telephone pick-up, organization within the office and the stores, the management of time and communication across job lines.

Length was specified at no more than 10 minutes. Shelf life was short: 6-9 months.

The key message was that everyone in the company was a part of a team, and the contribution of every single member mattered. 'Everything that everybody does affects the customer at some point.'

127

The tone was to be positive. 'Don't criticise the little people.'

DG also wished to encourage a pride in the company and the role of each individual within it, by emphasising their successes and demonstrating corporate commitments such as investment in new offices.

A slim but properly printed and bound book had been produced six months earlier. Entitled *Values and Objectives – Mission and Strategies*, it contained the policies and approach that DG was adopting throughout its European operations. It provided some background and some specific information to supplement the face-to-face brief.

DG's working language is English, and so the video was to be scripted and made in that language. There was a strong possibility, however, of translation into other languages.

Analysis

Two obvious hurdles had to be overcome. First, the wide cultural diversity of the audience (from Finland to Portugal) meant that any examples needed to be internationally understandable and acceptable. It was for this reason, plus the fact that the parent company is American, that the hook involved Columbus.

Second, the idea of 'Commitment to Excellence' had to be made visual. Once the bridge from the hook to the main body had introduced the idea of teamwork, it became a matter of showing instances of how excellence might be interpreted in a normal office environment.

The need to keep the tone positive meant that any bad example had to be offset by a good one.

A point that was of more significance to the director, but still had to be borne in mind for the script, was that locations – especially DG offices – should not be too readiliy identifiable as in one particular country. (Despite the fact that the West German DG subsidiary was the office that was to be used for filming.)

The Script

(Sounds of the sea, the
creaking of sailing ship
rigging)

(Library footage) Open ocean. Introduce pictures of early sailing ships.	
	12th October 1492.
Camera pans to reveal Caribbean island	
	The first landfall
(Library) Landing site	by Europeans in the New World
(Library) Pictures/paintings of early ships and seamen	A personal triumph
Superimpose, and then remove, name of Columbus	for one man –
	but the achievement was of his entire expedition
Pictures of specific skills at sea, such as navigation, shipwright, sailmaker, cook.	Ninety people working as a highly professional team, so that one could claim success – on behalf of them all.
Skyline of New York. Name of Columbus on screen Replace with Amerigo Vespucci Dissolve America out of Amerigo	And even then what he found wasn't named after him.
Busy (unidentified) offices	Businesses are much the same. Customers only ever see a few members of the company.
Customer in discussion with DG salesman	Salemen, perhaps,
	or engineers.
Engineer working on DG equipment	Yet they are buying products
Camera moves around busy DG office	to which *everyone* in the company has made a contribution. And unless that contribution is top quality, the products may not be.
Unsold hardware gathering dust	And so they may not be bought.

Mission statement in book Highlight key phrase DG office	So when we say our mission is to deliver complete solutions – 'complete' applies just as much to the *service* we provide as it does to the technology
Introduce visually in office environment the individual DG people who will feature in examples	And it's only people who can put in the little bit more that represents the difference between good and excellent - and the difference between us and our competitors.
Inside 'customer's' office. Customer's P.O.V. Pan from clock to diary entry showing DG visit at that time, to look up from desk to see DG person approaching. He/she smiles, moves to shake hands.	In very many cases, time is the key. When we are dealing directly with a customer, we know not to waste his time.
Manager at cluttered desk, talking on phone, trying to find papers, looking under files, puts briefcase on desk to look inside	But what about when we waste our own?
Move first image to half-screen. Introduce same manager, with tidier desk, also on phone. Expand to push first image off screen. Manager reaches for file, extracts paper he needs.	Being organized at a personal level is where a commitment to excellence starts.
Stores, not very well organized. Storeman frowning, looking for something, looking back at paper in his hand. Move first image to half-screen. Same storeman, now with more	And having our job organized

organized store, looks at
paper, as expand to push first
image off screen, goes straight
to what he is looking for
DG office interior

For everything that everybody
does has some effect on how
well we serve our customers.
Not just those in marketing,
say, or customer training, who
support sales directly.

Staff working at
terminals

That is why even those whose
work is completely internal
need the same level of
commitment –

Close-up of screen information
View across DG office, showing
different people in different
jobs

regardless of whether we are
in finance, personnel,
administration or information
management.

And the way we work within the
team is just as important.

People around a meeting room
table, obviously waiting;
coffee cups, looking at
watches. Head of table
empty. Door opens, manager
enters, sits down. Others order
their papers, get ready to
start, manager gets up for
a coffee, so they are still
left waiting.
Move to half-screen.
Introduce same setting, with
manager already sitting at
head of table preparing papers.
Expand to fill screen as those
attending meeting come in
Salesman and systems engineer
checking configuration of a
system.
Desk with no-one sitting at it

For then we can throw away
time in much larger
quantities.

When with a little thought we
could be making more of it.
In virtually anything we do.

Excellence is most of all an
attitude of mind
An approach which looks for

Close in on telephone

| | what *can* be done
| | rather than what can't.
Telephone rings. Pan to show | For example –
someone working at another | even if a telephone call
desk, ignoring it | isn't for us – it might be
| one of our customers – perhaps
| even our most important
| customer.

Move to half-screen. | So picking it up is only
Same setting. Person gets up | a first step.
from desk. Expand to fill
screen as phone is picked up.
Person shakes head, as if
saying 'they're not here',
doesn't offer to take message,
replaces phone.
Move to half-screen | Customer or colleague, any
Same setting. Person approaches | caller deserves the best that
ringing phone. Expand to fill | we can offer – and then just
screen as phone is picked up. | a little bit more.
Friendly approach, looks in
diary on desk, writes note for
absent person.

| As does *everything* we do.
| Not just for its own sake –
| but because individual
| excellence leads to team
| excellence.

Busy DG office | And when a team works well –
| and consistently well –
| success is likely to follow.

| As the Data General team in
| Europe has proved.

| And our own working
| surroundings start to reflect
Visual examples of new DG | that success – the outward
premises around Europe | signs of a company to be
| proud of.

	A company in which everybody's contribution is valued – because it matters.
Visual link to return to sea and early sailing-ship pictures	Businesses, like ships, only work well when everyone in them is thoroughly professional.
Sea captain	One person without a strong, high-quality team behind him is lost -
Stormy sea	sometimes, perhaps, even literally.
With upbeat music, re-show key images: the time in the diary and the prompt arrival of a salesman – the hand moving swiftly to a ringing telephone – the salesman and sales administrator working together – the storeman putting his hand immediately on what he needs – the manager ready to start a meeting promptly.	But people committed to excellence in whatever they do, both individually and as a team, can achieve remarkable results.
Reprise New York skyline Paris head office building	We can't discover America. But we *can* be the first in our own field.
Superimpose DG logo in the centre of the screen	And we can stay there.

Comment

The idea of Columbus and the analogy of teamwork in a ship was proposed and accepted early on. (The additional element of how one person gets the credit for everyone else's work – in the computer context, often the salesman – was found particularly appropriate.) The script was then developed through a full treatment stage. So the final script held few surprises for the client, and underwent comparatively few changes.

Apart from occasional amendments in terminology, and adjustments made by the director for ease of filming, there were thus only two important alterations. The voiceover reference to 'our competitors' was supported by visual representation of them, which was thought unnecessary emphasis and was deleted. And there was a short visual section showing some recent sales successes, in support of the voiceover talking about DG Europe's success as a team. It was removed to keep comfortably within the length specified. (The completed video lasted 9 minutes.)

Appendix C
An internal communication script

The Brief

The OCS Group draws its name from the initials of its biggest (although not its first) company, Office Cleaning Services. While nearly all the Group companies have the link between them of some connection with the care and maintenance of buildings, employees naturally identify more readily with the individual company they are with.

The object of the induction video was therefore to help new staff to feel part of the family of companies they had joined as soon as possible.

It needed to cover four elements. The first was the Group's history, which was worth the telling, since it had begun life in 1900. The second was the fact that it was still in family ownership, and the implications of that. The third was its philosophy, particularly towards its customers but also towards its staff. And the fourth was the make-up of the Group and the companies within it.

A 'book of the film' was prepared concurrently. The intention was that new employees would receive their personal copy of this booklet after they had seen the video. Each of the first three elements – the history, the family and the philosophy – would be in greater detail in the printed form, but be recognizably complementary. The history section of the book, for example, carried many of the same black-and-white archive stills that the video used.

The fourth element, the Group companies, was already available in brochure form.

The booklet also contained items such as pension and commission schemes which were originally planned for the video but soon identified as better suited to another medium.

A formula had to be found for the senior management of the Group to appear in person in the video, to welcome the new employees.

Analysis

Fascinating though the history was, much of it was anecdotal and detailed, and thus more suitable to the booklet. However, it provided a strong sideways hook and a logical bridge. Some archive material was available; other historical visuals had to come from library sources.

The philosophy had been originated for the booklet, and so was largely static. Without changing its content, a way had to be found to make it come alive a little more on the screen.

The director had worked with Group companies many times before. He was therefore very used to shooting appropriate shots for a visual line such as 'supervisor on site with customer' or 'general view, internal cleaning'. Little detailed visualization was therefore needed in those circumstances.

The Script

	Voiceover South Africa, 1899.
Rifle fire	
Shouts of soldiers	
Orders	
Military horses on the move.	War, between Britain and the
Introduce pictures of Boer	Boers.
War	The fighting lasted for three
	years. But it took only one
	year for a small London
General views of City *ca* 1900	shipping firm trading with

South Africa to be put out of
business.
One of their young managers
'Standard' picture of Frederick   was Frederick Goodliffe.
Goodliffe

He quickly turned his
attention to starting his own
business –
and he christened it for the
Early New Century pix, with   year of its founding, 1900.
name prominent
Early operational pictures   The New Century Window
Cleaning Company became the
the first of the many
customer-service companies
that have been brought
together since that time to
form the OCS Group of today.
Early OCS pictures   The next was Office Cleaning
Services, which was formed in
1930 and which would later
grow to be the largest Group
company.
Other diversification
followed – despite the
Eagle Street after bombing   intervention of the Second
World War.
Replacement Eagle Street   The expanding group moved
building   steadily into related fields
such as
Early Factory Cleaners pic   factory cleaning
Early Smarts pic   laundry
Early London Carpet Cleaners   carpet cleaning
pic

special finishes
Early Centuryan pic   and later on security,
and facilities management.
General internal cleaning,   One consistent idea running
window cleaning and security   through this pattern of
– modern footage   development, linking all the

group companies, is the care of buildings. But there are two others.

The first is that the Group should retain the advantages of being family-owned and -operated.

And it has done so.
As well as the Group still being a private organization, descendants of Frederick Goodliffe's eight children work in many of the Group companies –

'Gables' pic of Goodliffe family

Family tree, highlighting members who work in the business

the majority representing now the fourth generation of the family.
This continuity is equally true of the families of our staff, some of whom are in their second and third generation.
And there is continuity through long service, too.

Several representatives of different generations – arranged shot

Tankard

The tankard that marks 20 years of working in OCS Group has been presented over 500 times.

Tankard presentation montage

Being a nationwide group of companies means ample opportunity for promotion and relocation, and many members of staff have progressed from manual worker to director level.

The second constant is the Group's philosophy of working – that of putting the customer first.

	It may sound very simple.
	But it has to be worked at,
Customer pictures	because the future of all of
	us depends on it.
	That's why we see OCS Group
	not as the usual pyramid with
	the Chairman at the top, but
	one with our **customers** at
Inverted pyramid diagram	the top.
	Some of you will deal with
	those customers directly –
Staff on phone	on the phone,
Meeting customers	face-to-face,
Cleaning	or through the service you
	provide.
	But even if you're not dealing
	directly with our customers
Stores loading	yourself, your job is to help
Invoicing dept	someone who is.
Graphic sequence:	The customer, therefore, is
Triangle	given pride of place in our
Add 'customer' in centre	triangle of service.
	And at the points of the
	triangle are the three
	elements that make up our way
	of doing business.
Add 'strategy' at top	The needs and expectations of
	the customer provide us with
	our service strategy:
Superimpose 'Caring about a	caring about a reliable
reliable service', then fade	service.
all except 'service', which is	
flown to join 'strategy'	Our
Add 'delivery systems' bottom	delivery systems must make
left	good that promise of caring,
Duplicate 'service' from 'service	reliable service.
strategy', fly to add to	
'delivery systems'.	And
Add 'people' bottom right	our people must have the
	skills and the power to put it
	into practice.

Duplicate 'service' from 'service strategy', fly to add to 'people'

That's why we place a good deal of emphasis on training, which is run within each individual group company.

Training in progress, seen in at least two different group companies
Reprise complete triangle

This philosophy of service affects all of us at every point a customer comes into contact with any aspect of our organization.

Manager on telephone
Supervisor on site with customer
Visitor meeting security guard
Customer greeted by office receptionist
Split screen montage of close-up of OCS people in previous sequence

That's a moment of truth – when a customer forms an impression about the quality of the service we provide. Our aim must be to make every one of those impressions a good one. And that applies wherever we work in the Group

Substantial modern building. Freeze frame, fade to retain outline only. Use central space to show in turn typical activity of Division under discussion, then spin it out to a 'name-tag' position around edge of screen
Office cleaning
Window cleaning, jointly become
Cleaning Division
Laundry Division
Hygiene Division
Construction Division
Window Division
Security Division
Manufacturing Division

Virtually all the companies in the OCS Group have that same fundamental connection with buildings that began with Frederick Goodliffe's first company.

Cleaning, inside and out –

laundry, workwear, carpets and hygiene –

refurbishment and maintenance –
security –
manufacturing products to

Specialist Division (e.g. Throwers)
Overseas Division (European
map)

support the work of other
divisions –
facilities management
specialist activities –
and the provision of many of
the same services in other
countries.
The diversity of our
operations gives us a
marvellous opportunity to
grow

Graphic showing group services
outside building –
going in
= commission

by selling the services of
other group companies as an
addition to an existing
contract. And it's not only
good for the Group, it's good
for you – since we pay
commission on new business
you introduce.

Induction booklet

The details of that, and of
the Group's comprehensive
pension scheme, are contained
in this induction booklet.
In fact it will tell you a
good deal more than we've had
time to, about the Group
you've joined.

Early New Century pix

It is a Group that has grown
without a break from the
efforts of one man founding
a company, at the dawn of a
new century.

Key history landmarks – early
OCS, early Smarts

Group brochure, pages being
turned

But an established,
responsible, family-owned
business with locations
throughout the UK still has to
compete –
in a climate that gets

Close up of Frederick Goodliffe
portrait

Pull back from portrait, reveal
DHG, FDC and GHB sitting
around table.
As their discussion continues,
each one is seen virtually full
face, with name and position
caption. End on DHG, who once
identified turns full face to
camera.

Different angle: DHG now
flanked by FDC and GHB
OCS name and logo

tougher for service industries
all the time.
So the principles on which
Frederick Goodliffe built the
foundations of the OCS Group
apply
now more than they have ever
done.

DG We have to put the
customer first, too.
That way we can move with
confidence towards our own
new century.
Welcome to the OCS Group.

Comment

The close contact with the client was maintained through two
directors, who then sounded out other senior management within
the Group. The results of all those discussions, which were mostly
to make implicit points explicit or to improve emphasis, were then
distilled into one script revision. Given that those sort of changes
are bound to occur, it was a very painless way of doing them.

More substantial was the reshaping of the structure. In the first
draft, the three senior managers (in fact the Chairman, MD and
Deputy MD) were written in to appear at three different points in
the video. The words they were to speak, subsequently
incorporated into the voiceover, were part of the main narrative
of the video but tailored for them. On reflection, the decision was

taken to reduce their presence in the video to a much briefer section at the end, which was rewritten accordingly.

Although intended for new employees, and used as such, the video took on a secondary life almost immediately. Both the history and the philosophy proved to be of as much interest to clients as to employees – and there was also marketing value to be gained from demonstrating the quality of a video made purely for internal consumption.

A well-made video had therefore amply repaid the investment in it. As it always will.